What People Are Saying About *Disney Magic: Business Strategy You Can Use at Work and at Home*

Loaded with information and easy to read! Rich Hamilton has combined stories about Walt Disney with useful success methods that Disney used to create Disneyland. If you like Disneyland, or have ever wondered how Walt Disney came up with the idea and successfully put the business together, read this book.

—Jim Cathcart, Author,
The Eight Competencies of Relationship Selling

Rich Hamilton captures the essential quality of Disney's genius. You're given a rare opportunity of stepping inside the mind of a visionary by exploring the dimensions of Walt Disney's dreams. This book is a "must read" for anyone seriously striving to obtain personal or professional success.

— Carole Copeland Thomas, Syndicated Radio Personality

Rich Hamilton helps with more than selling and marketing, he knows how to deliver on a dream, plan complex projects, and put together a responsive workforce. Listen carefully to what Rich says about engineering a successful business.

—Bill Brooks, Author, *High Impact Selling*

Rich Hamilton insists that we can all succeed by applying a few simple methods. Rich's down-to-earth way of looking at business is refreshing. Hamilton is at his best when discussing such specifics as how to give people what they want, how to understand promotion, and how to generate follow-up business.

—James Malinchak, Author, *From College to the Real World*

D0933068

Disney Magic

Business Strategy
You Can Use at Work
And at Home

*"My business is making people,
especially children, happy."*
—Walt Disney

*Be a person of imagination and dreams. Follow a plan to
make your dreams come true. Enjoy immensely successful
projects. Organize a happy, motivated team and make a
difference in the world. This is my wish for you.*

Rich Hamilton

SellBetter Tools
Phoenix, Arizona, USA

Disney Magic

First Edition
Copyright © 2003 Rich Hamilton. All Rights Reserved.

ISBN 0-9728476-0-X
Library of Congress Control Number: 2003090922

Publisher's Cataloging-in-Publication Data
(Prepared By Cassidy Cataloguing Services, Inc.)

Hamilton, Rich.

   Disney magic : business strategy you can use at work and at home / Rich
   Hamilton. — 1st ed. — Phoenix, Ariz. : SellBetter Tools, 2003.

      p. ; cm.

   Includes bibliographical references.
   ISBN 0-9728476-0-X

   1. Success in business. 2. Management. 3. Business planning. 4. Strategic
   planning. 5. Walt Disney Company.

HF5386 .H36 2003   2003090922
650.1—dc21   CIP

Disclaimer: While every precaution has been taken in the preparation of this
book, the publisher and author assume no responsibility for errors or omissions.
Neither is any liability assumed for damages resulting, or alleged to result,
directly or indirectly from the use of the information contained herein. If you do
not wish to be bound by the above, you may return this book with receipt to the
publisher for a full refund of the purchase price.

Schools and Corporations: This book is available at quantity discounts with
bulk purchases for educational or business use. For more information please
contact the publisher at the address below.

SellBetter Tools
Box 50186, Phoenix, AZ 85076 • 1-888-240-4742

Manufactured in the United States of America

Contents

A Note to Management

As you reflect on what you read here, you may think that Disney has used modern management techniques that everyone should know. The difference here is that at Disney theme parks, they actually do it! And it works.

Too often, it seems, a new initiative is introduced at the annual conference, or a training program or retreat is used with the hope that communication and productivity will be improved. For a moment, there is hope. But by the next Monday morning you realize nothing has really changed.

Here's the challenge: Today and every day you are competing with the very best. No matter what your product or service, your customers and your employees compare you with the best run companies in the universe. One of those is Disney, and they experience Disney best at the theme parks where the customer experience is superb and the employee satisfaction... well, they have a high percentage of employees who stay there for decades.

A Note to Everyone Else

How can it make sense to learn about Disney's theme park business when you work in a job where someone else has control of the business? The business strategies that Disney uses in its theme parks are powerful methods that can be applied in your job and at home.

In this volume, you will discover specific methods you can use on the job to be more effective and to get more done. You'll find your job is more fun, and you'll come to work more excited. Over time, others in your company may adopt some of these methods, and the resulting synergy will benefit you all.

You will also find specific things you can do at home to make your time with your family more fun and more productive. You'll be a double winner, at work and at home.

And, if your company's management gave you this book, you may be lucky enough to be part of a company where they are adopting these methods. That means you have the opportunity to be part of a very special transformation, as your company becomes more dynamic and more fun.

Acknowledgments

Writing this book would not have been possible without the help and assistance of some very special people.

Thanks to Larry Winget, who told me to load the book with good information and still keep it under 100 pages so it's quickly and easily read. We've accomplished that.

And to Mark Victor Hansen, who assured me this book would have massive value in the marketplace, thanks.

I thank Nancy Yeamans, Ph.D., Rick Hubbard, D.Cs., Ken Pollock, Ph.D., and Susan Pollock, Ph.D., ABAP, who read early drafts of the manuscript and provided valuable questions and suggestions.

Thanks to colleagues Jim Cathcart, Bill Brooks, Carole Copeland Thomas, John Hersey, Ted Risch, Christine Harvey, Greg Godek, James Malinchak, Rod Rademacher, Rob McKnight, and Richard Davis for their encouragement and advice.

Bill Leonard, who recently retired as editor of the editorial page at the *Des Moines Register,* deserves a very special thank you; in 1966, as a night editor at *The Hutchinson News,* Bill struggled with this young, hopeful writer, teaching me newspaper style and admonishing me to keep asking pertinent questions.

Thanks also goes to editors Wayne Lee, Jim Hitch, Don Kendall, and Stuart Awbrey, to publisher Peter Macdonald, and to journalism teacher Aylene Keown; they coached me and coaxed me many years ago into writing.

To those who ventured with me to Disneyland and Walt Disney World, Bill and Carole Agard, Claudia Hose, Steve Hose, Ira and Robyn Emus, Tony Vicich, Randy Stephenson, Chip and Pat Rollins, Ron and Lyn Dressler, Susan Moffitt, Jim Golden, thanks for the insight. To the "kids," Brian, Curt, Karen, Kysa, Rachel, Noah, David, Alishia, and Nicole, thanks for letting me live the magic through your eyes.

Thanks to my parents, Martha and Dick, who not too long ago twice bravely ventured with me to Disneyland, including a wet and cold expedition for the grand opening of California Adventure.

To the hundreds of Disney cast members who answered my unending questions, and to those who demonstrated the magic, thanks for the adventure.

To Marcy Cummins, who said, "Write," and her husband, Joe, who said, "Right!"

Some have passed on, but were alive in my heart as this book became a reality.

To my wife, Sharon, a very special thank you. Accompanying me repeatedly to Disneyland, she watched and occasionally agonized as I examined the Disney business and asked questions about the organization. It was my idea to study the business model, but it was her idea that I should write the book. A writer herself, she read and reread the manuscript, editing the manuscript and assisting in uncountable ways.

Finally, to Walt Disney, who lived it and made it happen: Thanks!

Preface–A Note to the Reader

You, like me, have probably visited a Disney theme park.

At seven years old I watched Disneyland open on television from the comfort of my distant Midwest home. Thirty-one years later I made my first personal visit.

I prepared for that visit for many years.

In grade school the neighbor kids, my cousins and I joined as avid television "members" of *The Mickey Mouse Club,* complete with Mickey, Minnie, Donald and Daisy, and joined by Spin and Marty, the Hardy Boys, and the energetic Mouseketeers.

We all took time to watch Walt Disney's weekly *Disneyland, Walt Disney Presents,* and *Disney's Wonderful World of Color* television programs, with the variety of live action, nature, science, and animated features. As Disneyland expanded, Walt Disney himself described the new attractions, and we were all duly amazed at the remarkable goings-on in Anaheim.

Eventually some of my cousins actually went to Disneyland as part of a family vacation. Home movies of them riding in spinning teacups, flying on elephants, and swimming in the pool at the Disneyland Hotel, proved that there really was a magical place where everyone could have a good time.

Walt Disney started his career in the heart of America, not California, but in Kansas City just a few hours drive from my home. A biography I read in the eighth grade told of Walt's challenges getting started in animation, and I learned that his entire life had been a struggle as he advanced the art and science of animation and movies. Little was said in that old biography about television or theme parks.

When I made my first visit to Disneyland that busy day in 1986, I was prepared for a magical experience. But I discovered more than a return to childhood fantasy. My business personality suddenly was estimating the crowd (at 30,000) and multiplying that times the daily ticket price, adding in meals, toys, sweatshirts, silly hats, and a few churros, and considering the gross sales at some two and one-half million dollars a day!

It's Different

Like me, you've probably been to other amusement parks. But Disney is different. They look different, they act different. There are more people there. And those guests behave differently, and spend more.

I started looking around at how the business was run. I wondered what the business secrets were. I wondered how things worked. I wondered what I could learn that I could apply to my personal life, my work, and my business.

I decided to visit Disneyland often, and now I visit the park many times each year. I ask questions. I read everything. I watch how things are handled. This book is the result of that quest.

Picture this. Disney's US theme parks. Sixty-five thousand employees. Eighty per cent of those come into direct contact with customers. Success depends on those 65,000 people providing service that delights customers. Disney pulls it off, perhaps better than any other sizeable organization on Earth.

A Unique Way to Look at Disney

I must point out that I've never worked for the Walt Disney Company, although I'd love to have them as a client. I've never taken their formal training at the Disney Institute or elsewhere, although I understand it's outstanding. I'm not a stockholder, although I might change that someday, and some mutual funds I own might give me an indirect investment.

So what qualifies me to write this book? Thirty-some years of consulting and advising hundreds of businesses regarding marketing and advertising. A considerable investment with Disney as a customer. Research and informal interviews with cast members. And I paid a *lot* of attention.

You're going to learn what I discovered, not the official company story. Much of what you'll find here is pure Disney. Much is my interpretation, balanced with my business and consulting experience. This book is not authorized in any way by The Walt Disney Company. They may approve of much that I write here. Some they may not like, particularly when I point out what they're doing wrong.

You see, there were some interesting principles established in the early days by Walt Disney and his brother Roy. Those principles led to many successes and a few failures, and brought powerful systems to the Disney operation, some devised by the Disneys, and many created and implemented by Disney employees. Today, long after the deaths of Walt and Roy, the company survives, but when it violates those key principles it does so at great cost.

I also discovered some interesting differences between Disneyland and Walt Disney World. The Florida venture is bigger, comprising four major theme parks plus other shopping and recreation areas, hotels, and a complete community. As a result, some things that work informally in California are formalized in Florida, and there are more operational differences than I expected. Also, Disney is a moving target; they're constantly experimenting and evolving.

Still, the principles are similar, and I hope I've extracted the ideas in ways they will be useful.

Where I've succeeded, the real credit belongs to Walt Disney, his brother Roy, and the amazing employees at The Walt Disney Company. I may look at certain things differently than they do, but I think my interpretations are valid and useful. Where I may have erred, I apologize; the error is all mine.

How This Book Will Help You

Here's my promise: Read this book. Apply the methods and strategies covered here. You will be able to take these principles and apply them to your personal life, to your work, and to your company.

I expect this book to have equal application for business managers, their employees, and outside business in personal life.

You'll find stories about Walt Disney, and about Disneyland, and most important, about the application of these principles away from Disneyland.

The book was written for two groups of people, and, really, you're probably in both groups. Most of the "magic" principles will apply to you at home, and at work.

It's been my observation that most people who have it together in one area usually have it together in both home and business. So, apply these principles at home, and at work. Eventually you'll need it to run the business, the department, or the organization.

Commitment

Walt Disney was able to make dreams come true. You can, too, when you have established your values, you believe in yourself, and you commit to begin the process.

Do you want to make your life better? Choose to put magic in your own life by copying the following information onto a piece of paper and signing the commitment:

Magic In Your Life Commitment

I hereby decide to put magic in my life so I can determine my dreams and make them come true.

Signed this _____ day of _____, 20_____.

By_____*(your signature)*_____.

As a further demonstration of your commitment please go to our special internet website and register your decision:

www.MagicStrategy.com

I will email you a certificate of commitment recognizing this important first step. (Look for the "Commitment" button, and use the access code 1313. Later in this book, you'll learn the significance of that code number.)

Next time you're at Disneyland or Walt Disney World, watch to see how this all works. It's amazing! And while you're there, if you see me, be sure to say hello.

—*Rich Hamilton*

Walt Disney's Formula that Makes Dreams Come True

"WHEN YOU WISH upon a star…" begins the song used as a theme for Disney television programs, and, perhaps, a theme for the entire Disney operation.

Walt Disney was a man of dreams. He dreamed big dreams. And he made his dreams come true.

Walt Disney would agree, and is himself ample proof, that dreams can come true. His example reveals that making dreams come true takes more than just wishing. In Walt's case, the "star" was Mickey Mouse, and combined with a lot of vision, planning, and hard work, Walt made dream after dream come true.

Most people think of Walt Disney as an animator, the "inventor" of Mickey Mouse. He is more accurately thought of as an entertainer, not in the sense that he wanted to be the center of attention, but that he wanted to create something that would excite an audience and make them laugh.

Walt had talent, and developed a keen commercial sense of what would appeal to the public. This combination enabled him to parlay $40 and a few drawing tools into a film studio producing popular cartoons, feature length animated features, and live action movies.

Disneyland, Walt Disney World, and ultimately the other Disney theme parks around the world all came about because Walt Disney insisted that he could build an amusement park that was so much bigger and better than other amusement parks that it shouldn't even be called an amusement park.

How did this dream come about?

As a child in Kansas City, Walt watched through the fence at Fairmont Park, wanting to participate, but not having enough money to enter.

A parent in the 1930's, Walt would take his children to amusement parks. But he was not amused, convinced he could do much better. By 1937, at the premiere of *Snow White*, Walt told Wilfred Jackson that someday he would "make a park for kids, a place scaled down to kid size."

In 1940 he revealed a plan to showcase "Disney characters in their fantasy surroundings"[1] at a park across the street from the Disney studio in Burbank.

The vision of an amusement park grew in Walt's mind as he traveled through the US and Europe and visited attractions of all kinds. He visited county fairs, state fairs, circuses, carnivals, and parks. He was distressed at operations where things were run down and ride operators were hostile. And he loved the spotless Tivoli Gardens in Copenhagen, with bright, upbeat music, excellent food and drink, and warm, friendly employees.

Walt was convinced that an amusement park would be successful in the United States if it offered a "good show" that families could enjoy together, was clean, and had friendly employees.

In 1948 he shared his concept with trusted friends, a modest amusement park with a central village including a town hall, a small park, railroad station movie theater, and small stores. Outlying areas would include a carnival area and a western village. Soon he added spaceship and submarine rides, a steamboat, and exhibit halls.

Four years later, in 1952, he decided on "Disneyland" for the name and formed a company to develop the park, Disneyland, Inc.

Walt's brother Roy, the studio's financial head, was against investing in Disneyland. Bankers and amusement industry experts forecast doom. That's why Walt stepped outside the studio organization to develop the idea. Eventually Roy agreed to help, and the Disney studio became part of the operation.

In 1953 Walt brilliantly strategized combining television production with development of the park. The *Disneyland* television program on ABC had a dual benefit. It promoted the new park through a weekly program, and it became part of a deal where the network invested half a million dollars plus substantial loan guarantees in return for a 35% ownership in Disneyland Park.

That same year he enlisted Stanford Research Institute to examine the economic prospects of Disneyland (it was deemed profitable) and to find the ideal location (Anaheim).

They broke ground in July, 1954, and one year later, on July 17, 1955, Disneyland opened.

Within 7 weeks, a million visitors had visited Disneyland, making it one of the biggest tourist attractions in the US. Attendance was 50 per cent ahead of predictions and guests were spending 30 per cent more than expected.

Walt combined his talent and his sense of what the public would want with lots of hard work. Today we might call him a "workaholic." His work was driven, not by guilt or insecurity, but by a dream. As he told an interviewer in 1955: "Everybody can make their dreams come true. It takes...a dream – faith in it – and hard work. But that's not quite true because it's so much fun you hardly realize it's work."[2]

At a dinner party at Herb Ryman's house in 1960, someone commented that Walt could be elected president if he wanted it. His response? "Why would I want to be President of the United States? I'm the King of Disneyland!"[3]

In 1960, after 37 years in Hollywood, with a mixture of huge successes and frustrating setbacks, Disney had created something that was successful beyond Walt's own dreams. With Disneyland and its continuing stream of visitors, Walt had finally achieved financial stability.

Keys to Making Your Own Dreams Come True

Walt Disney had big dreams. Do your dreams have to be as big? Here's some really exciting news: It's entirely up to you!

In this book you'll find a number of extremely valuable ideas and strategies that will help you live a magical life, and build a remarkable business. But none of them will mean anything unless you first have a dream and know how to put it into action.

Have you ever experienced this? You are summoned to a big meeting, or a staff meeting, or a pep rally. You're told there's a "new plan," and everything will be wonderful for everyone. Perhaps there's a new campaign theme, or a new slogan, or maybe the company even changed their name. Maybe there's new management, or a new coach, or the cheerleaders have a new cheer.

Everything seems wonderful for awhile, maybe even all day, but by next week things are back to "normal." And "normal" isn't very good.

You see, that's how things go in most organizations, and here's why it happens. It's because everyone wants to be part of a big dream, one that they believe in and want to achieve. But most organizations don't have a very good dream, and they don't communicate it very well, and they don't execute it very well.

Failing that, a company, school, or other group throws a nice party, but realizes little long term benefit.

Walt Disney knew how to dream, and he knew how to share that dream with his organization so it worked. With Walt, it was personal, and he carried the message to his organization.

Since Walt's death in 1966, The Walt Disney Company makes the message live in their theme parks and developed systems that make everyone part of the dream. In this book, you're going to learn how to do that very thing. You can apply it to your business, and you can apply it to your personal life.

Here's how you start. There are several keys to realizing your dreams that become apparent when you study the life of Walt Disney:

1. Think. Walt shows us the first step towards success is to think about your values and to become well-centered on who you are.

Walt spent formative childhood years on a farm near Marceline, Missouri. His parents were religious and hard working, struggling to survive. There, and later helping his father deliver papers, Walt learned to respect hard work, honesty, and Midwestern values. He also learned determination and persistence, and became motivated to succeed.

2. Believe. The first thing you realize about Walt Disney was that he personifies a can-do attitude. Walt grew up in poverty, but was determined to prosper, to make a positive mark on the world. He never listened to those who suggested he would not succeed. He was confident that he would find a way.

Disneyland has a music and fireworks presentation called "Believe! There's Magic in the Stars!" It reflects the idea that you must have complete faith in your ability to accomplish what you want.

One of the greatest attributes of the human condition is our ability to lift ourselves out of our current situation and do something bigger and better than anything we've done before. Many people demonstrate that ability, some in small, personal ways, some with spectacular success. Walt Disney is one of those who produced spectacular success, again and again.

The universe demonstrates unlimited abundance. Scientists have yet to find the outer edge of the universe, and they theorize that it's expanding, growing. Our planet is constantly bombarded with energy, from the sun, from the stars, and from throughout the universe. There is constant, unlimited energy available; we only have to know how to harness it.

And the key to harnessing energy is an idea, the kernel of a dream, launched into reality.

3. Dream. This key is self-evident, to make dreams come true, you must have dreams.

You, like me, might wonder about this. When I first started looking at the idea of dreams, I thought dreams were the same as fantasies. It seemed impractical to dream; I thought it was best to pick practical goals, those within reach.

Walt Disney helps you and me resolve this because he made the "impossible" possible. He added sound to cartoons. He added color. He produced the first feature-length animated film, *Snow White*. And he created Disneyland.

Another important point: Have more than one dream! Have big and little dreams. Have personal and business dreams.

Write them down. Make a list of your dreams. Review and add to it regularly. Set priorities, and decide which of your dreams mean most to you. Then you can focus on what's important.

4. Dare to let your dreams grow and become urgent. Walt's Disneyland dream started small, a simple idea for a better amusement park. It grew and took form. In the process, over a period of at least 15 years, it became bigger and more precise.

This is important for you, too. Just as you are learning, growing, and becoming the future "you," your dream, if it's worthy, will grow and become more defined.

It takes vision. Think of each of your dreams in a variety of ways. In your mind, picture how it will look when it happens. Listen to what you will hear. Imagine how it will feel. As you let your mind create these impressions the dream will become more powerful, and you will be better able to accomplish what needs to be done.

First, Walt thought there could be a better amusement park. Before long, he started to think he should build it. Walt was going to build a small park in Burbank, an attraction for people who came to tour the Disney studios. Eventually, he knew the park should be much larger and he had to find a better location.

5. **Give your dream a name.** It seems so simple, yet it carries tremendous strength.

Walt's dream became much more powerful when he first gave it a name. First it was an idea for an amusement park, and then, in 1948, he gave it a name, "Mickey Mouse Park." Other names he toyed with around that time included "Disneylandia" and "Walt Disney's America."

Of course, eventually he settled on Disneyland, but the point here is simple: When you give your dream a name, it takes on a life of its own.

Even as the dream was growing, and the name changed, he was able to think and talk about it as a "real" entity or thing.

He could talk to his older brother, Roy, about Mickey Mouse Park, explain his ideas and share his enthusiasm. As with most of Walt's other big, expensive ideas over the years, Roy opposed the concept, which probably challenged Walt to pursue it even more.

6. **"Be sure you're right and then go ahead."** The saying, made famous in Disney's Davy Crockett television and movie features in the 1950's, was a part of the Disney formula, although Walt might not have vocalized it with those words.

Because Roy opposed Walt every time he dreamed a new, expensive venture, Walt was forced to examine the idea carefully. Walt was persistent and would push Roy as long as necessary in order to win approval. In the process the idea would evolve. Walt had to make sure the project was consistent with his values, that the public would respond and that the project would benefit the company and its customers.

Walt was a dreamer; there were probably projects that were dropped because he was unable to justify them to his brother.

7. **Set a goal.** It's been said that a goal is a dream with a date attached, but it's much more than that.

A goal is a combination of your faith in your abilities and your belief in the worth of the dream. By setting a date, you declare your intention to deliver on your dream, to turn it from a dream to a reality.

As your dream grows, set a date for it's realization. Once that's done, you're ready to lay out a plan and begin its execution.

8. **Lay out a detailed plan.** Walt drew and redrew plans for the park for years. Finally it was time to go into action.

Herb Ryman, a former animator, was asked to meet Walt at the studio one Saturday morning in 1953. "We're going to do an amusement park," Walt told him. "Roy is going to New York Monday morning to meet with the bankers. Roy has to show them what this place is going to look like."

"Well, I'd like to see what this place is going to look like, too," Ryman said. "Where have you got all this stuff?"

"You're going to do it," Walt answered. Walt stayed with him through the weekend, describing what he wanted Disneyland to look like. Ryman completed an aerial schematic of the proposed park by Monday morning.

Disneyland had been precisely defined for the first time, and the new brochure proclaimed, "Sometime in 1955, Walt Disney will present for the people of the world—and children of all ages— a new experience in entertainment."[4]

The funding was obtained, plans were completed, and work began.

What about your dream? Write a description and draw pictures or diagrams that will help you and anyone else who is helping you to visualize what's going to happen.

Imagine the process necessary to achieve your dream and draw up a step-by-step plan. Break the process into small, easy to accomplish steps.

For each step in your plan, write down what needs to happen.

Then set a date for completion of each step, creating an interim goal, or mini-goal. In this way, the list of mini-goals becomes more than a plan, it's a scoreboard that lets you keep track of your progress.

9. **Bring others in to help.** When it was time to get started, Walt assembled some of the top artists from the studio and moved them to a special company, WED Enterprises, to plan the park. They studied other amusement parks, and examined Disney cartoons for ideas to use in attractions. That group is now called Disney Imagineering, reflecting the emphasis on imagination.

Walt knew he couldn't do it all himself, even though he probably wanted to. Walt believed, "You can dream, create, design,
and build the most wonderful place in the world, but it requires
people to make the dream a reality.[5]" And Walt had a magical
method of bringing out the best in his people and himself, a
process used extensively in movies and television today. It's called
"storyboarding," and it serves to focus everyone's energy on
possible outcomes.

The practical side of all this is dependent on the dream. If you're
building a Disneyland, like Walt, it takes lots of people.

While bringing in others to help, Walt would not sanction in-
competence. A perfectionist, he found it difficult to tolerate in-
competence even while someone was learning a task. Still, he
would nurture someone as they learned, then insisting on competence from others, just as he did for himself.

Walt was also quick to bring in outside firms as partners or as
sponsors on projects he wanted to develop. He developed four
exhibits at the 1964-65 World's Fair in New York for Ford Motor
Co., General Electric, State of Illinois, and Pepsi-Cola. Most were
moved later to Disneyland.

If your dream is to redecorate your bedroom, you may want to
collaborate with friends who have redecorated, or with an inte-
rior designer, or with a consultant at the paint store.

10. Take action. Walt Disney formed Disneyland, Inc., on his own,
without initial support from the Disney studio because his
brother Roy opposed the project. He started two other
organizations to help design and build attractions and to develop
park plans.

He used his top artists and set designers to design the buildings
and décor, and brought in a large architectural and engineering
firm to design the buildings.

Construction was started with a completion date, and grand
opening just a year later, an impossible deadline.

He had attractions assembled, in part, at the studio and trans-
ported them to Anaheim. He brought in an experienced land-
scaper to clear and shape the land and to plant trees to create
the look of an established area.

11. Be persistent. Even with a plan, things go wrong. Even with
enthusiasm, obstacles are found.

Engineers planned a water tower for Disneyland to supply pressure for fire hydrants and sprinklers. Walt thought that would be ugly. "Find another solution," he ordered, and they piped water in from more than one source, affording sufficient pressure.

His planners worked six days a week, and Walt was right there with them, and sometimes did the designing himself. Disneyland became a crusade for Walt, even more than his pioneering work in animation.

12. **Evaluate and adapt.** Evaluate the results as you take action and adapt your plans and your actions so you can still meet your goals.

As your dream continues to grow and even after you have started work toward your goal, like Walt's, your goal may need to be revised. He had to set and reset goals for park design, creating new and bigger attraction ideas, financing, and more.

His original plan included a "land" called Lilliputan Land, with tiny mechanical figures. Walt needed time to develop the technology to make them move.

The Jungle Cruise was planned with live animals, but they sleep and hide much of the time; the ride was changed to mechanical animals so guests get a good look on every trip.

The castle, originally planned quite large, was scaled down and turned around to give it a friendly, storybook appearance and so it would not be visible from adjoining areas.

Though presented here as 12 distinct keys, they are not really a magic step-by-step formula. Walt probably never had a list of steps, though he would probably tell you "Think, Believe, Dream, and Dare."[6] Examination of his work reveals these keys in much of his work.

It's a process that starts with the individual – you – and moves through the creation and production of a project.

Obstacles are No Obstacle

ENTERTAINING? Yes, but I was puzzled after my first visit to the Haunted Mansion at Disneyland. I loved the ride and the amazing effects inside. But, as I looked back, I thought that Disney had overcome physical reality.

The Haunted Mansion is a nice big house, but it's nowhere near as big as the ride inside.

As I thought about it, I remembered that once inside, we entered a room and were lowered to basement level. But as I looked back at the building, I could see that there still wasn't enough room to bury that big ride in that little hill.

Later, leaving Disneyland, I drove around the perimeter and saw a big, light green building on the west side of the grounds. I figured out that the ride is outside the park, outside the "berm" that holds the Disneyland Railroad tracks. Disney engineers had put the ride outside, and the mansion itself is just an entrance that lets you go to the lower level, walk under the railroad, and load into the ride.

They had a big ride for Disneyland, but no room to build it; this was their novel solution.

Of course, Walt Disney had faced obstacles before, and he made overcoming obstacles part of the corporate culture.

In 1922, when Walt first started Laugh-O-Gram Films in Kansas City, he ran into money problems when customers didn't pay him as expected. He was forced into bankruptcy just a year later.

He overcame that setback by moving to California with just $40 in cash, a checkered coat, pants that didn't match, and some drawing materials. And he started again.

In Hollywood, he started producing cartoons. By 1928, he was turning out the popular Oswald the Lucky Rabbit cartoons at a brisk pace. But he lost the contract with the distributor, and, since Walt didn't own rights to the character, he lost that, too, and most of his animators left to continue producing Oswald.

Not willing to give up, he started over, this time with a mouse.

When Disneyland opened, Walt thought youngsters would drive the small cars in the original Autopia ride and learn respect for one another and the rules of the road. Within a couple of weeks, most of the cars had been destroyed by children who loved smashing into one another. The ride was changed.

A live circus, originally part of Walt's concept, was quietly dropped as problems grew and crowds showed little interest.

So many people went to Disneyland that the lines got too long. It created a negative impression and clogged up the park. Long lines were made to look shorter by using a snakelike pattern back and forth in parallel lines, and adding a variety of visual images and audio surprises as a sort of "pre-show" entertainment. This made standing in line more pleasant.

Walt told an engineer, "You know better than to kill an idea without giving it a chance to live. We set our sights high. That's why we accomplish so many things. Now go back and try again."[7]

Walt Disney once said, "There's really no secret about our approach. We keep moving forward—opening new doors and doing new things—because we're curious. And curiosity keeps leading us down new paths. We're always exploring and experimenting... we call it Imagineering—the blending of creative imagination and technical know-how."[8]

How to Use this at Home and at Work

Life demonstrates that once you start to deliver on a dream, something will happen to make it more difficult than expected.

It's been said the true measure of your character is not determined by what happens to you, for many things will happen. Real character is demonstrated by how you react to what happens.

Walt said "try again and again." When obstacles appear, learn to adapt and "find another way."

How to Use this in Your Company

When I first managed a radio station, it seemed that every project we undertook required more time and effort than we expected. Over time, I discovered that most projects took about three times as long as I might estimate. From that time on, if there was a job that "should" take 10 hours to produce, I planned on 30. I just multiplied everything by three. It was remarkably accurate.

Walt sometimes ran into what appeared to be insurmountable obstacles, but each time he overcame them.

His pattern was simple. He refused to admit defeat, and learned to "find another way." He would accept certain losses (the loss of Oswald), but find a way to overcome that loss with something better (the Mouse).

This optimistic approach to handling setbacks is a major part of his success. He was persistent, and would try again and again until he "found another way."

The Amazing Secret of How Everyone Gets the Big Picture

ONE ITEM REMAINED on our list. Our Disneyland trip was nearly over. Our son had requested we find a Goofy watch for his wife; her favorite character is Goofy, and she wanted a Goofy watch that runs backwards.

We stopped at the watch shop in Main Street, U.S.A., but didn't see a watch that looked like the one we needed.

It had been a busy day in the park, and lots of guests were still around. The shop was so full, it was difficult to look through the glass cases at the selection. A friendly face behind the counter asked if she could help us find something special.

"Sure," I said. "We're leaving for home in the morning, and we're looking for an adult Goofy watch, the kind that turns backward."

"I know the watch you want, and I'm not sure whether we have one," she responded. "Did you look in this case over here?"

She found several Goofy watches, but not the one we wanted. This amazing woman didn't stop there. She checked two more cases. Then she looked in a storage cabinet. Finally she said, "I know how frustrating it can be to want something and not be able to find it. Since it looks like you don't want to switch to one of the other Goofy watches, is it okay if I take the time to make a phone call?"

We waited while she called three other stores, including one at the Disneyland Hotel, looking for that watch. Finally she called the warehouse to see if there were any in stock there.

Showing true concern, she apologized and gave us a toll-free phone number we could call when we got home. "Sometimes they can supply you with park products. If not, maybe it will be available next time you're here; I know it's a popular model, but we never know what they're going to stock."

Although this incident ended in failure, I contrasted it with other efforts to buy specific products in stores at home. Seldom have I seen this much effort or concern for a customer wanting to buy an inexpensive gift.

While it's not seen often elsewhere, it's pretty common in a Disney theme park.

On my next visit to the park I was looking for a specific Mickey Mouse train. The store was out, but the person I asked called around and found a train at another store. I thanked this Disney merchandiser, and told her about the previous experience with the watch.

"I don't often see this major effort to help the customer on the 'outside,'" I said, "but I often see it here at Disneyland. How is it that Disney makes it happen so well?"

"It's part of our training," she answered. "We take pride in helping you find what you want, because we want you to have a magical experience here."

"Does it always work?" I asked.

"Sadly, some of us won't do it, but most of us will. It's really what Disney is all about, part of the 'magic.' We have to look at the 'big picture,' and do whatever is required to help a guest have a smile on his face."

I thought about that, and realized that the Disney organization has successfully established a remarkable corporate culture.

At the Disney studio, and later at Disneyland, Walt Disney was the primary motivator and expediter. He set the direction and the pace.

Generally, Walt knew exactly what he wanted. He insisted on creating a certain image, and delivering a special experience. His presence established a wonderful creative atmosphere, fostering a highly productive, highly charged work force.

Every member of the Disney staff worked under the "Disney system," and if they didn't agree with the way Walt wanted to do business, Walt figured they shouldn't be there.

When Walt was running Disney, his dream was the company vision, and he evangelized it to everyone. Walt called it "the whole package."

Today the company wants every employee to understand "The Big Picture." What's the big picture?

Disney's "Service Theme"

Roy Disney opposed building Disneyland because he looked at the business as the "movie business." Walt had a broader idea, which defined the business and established the criteria for where he was going. Walt said, "My business is making people, especially children, happy."[9] Shortly after Disneyland opened, Disneyland University was created to teach the Disney system to all the new people. Disney defines its business with a simple mission statement which it calls a "service theme." In 1955, at Disney University, it was simply, "We create happiness."[10]

Since then, it's evolved slightly, and today the controlling service theme is:

"We create happiness by providing the finest in entertainment for people of all ages, everywhere."

This provides the foundation of what they do. It applies to all business activity, to attractions, to stores, and to hotels. And it applies at all levels, from top management to support staff.

From this foundation, they expand with their history of innovation and show business success. At Disney, they recognize that Disney films and theme parks have grown to mean certain things in terms of image, subject, cleanliness, morality, and entertainment value.

So they've defined what they expect in terms of appearance, behavior, and achievement. And they expect every employee to be a part of it.

In the process, they've developed some interesting psychology and expectations to make it happen. Let's take a look:

The Finest in Family Entertainment

Disney represents entertainment.

Disney appeals to all ages.

Disney means fun, excitement, and quality.

A Unique Language

Disney's culture taps its show business roots, and the language they use reflects this.

Employees are called cast members, performers, and hosts.

Customers are called guests.

Cast members create a show every day for the guests.

They have a role to play in the show, not a job. They wear costumes, not uniforms. They perform to the audience. "Onstage" means being within sight of the guests.

When things are working right, it's a "good show."

Having their own language helps reinforce the unique company culture.

Every Guest is a V.I.P.

Guests are the top priority.

People expect the best from Disney, and the goal is to exceed expectations.

The company wants the people who visit Disney parks treated as guests, not customers. Each guest is to be treated as a guest arriving at a party, with unique needs and expectations. The cast members who work at an attraction in the park are called attraction hosts. It can be argued that some people don't know how to treat a customer, but they know how to treat a guest.

Friendly Employees

Cast members uphold the Disney Image.

They create happiness for guests.

They make conversation individual for each guest.

They talk to children on their own level.

Know the Answers

Guests expect cast members to know Disney history and trivia, company information, product information, ride information, and park hours.

Cast members who do not know the answer should know where to get the answer, and get it for the guest.

Disciplines of the Show

Cast members work while guests play.

The show must go on; when busy, remain calm, in control, and communicate.

The Applause

Guests applaud cast members with a smile, a wave, or a thank you.

The company applauds cast members with an award program.

Other Parts of the Culture

The Disney culture includes working toward common goals, like keeping the resort clean and litter-free. That means everyone, senior executives and front line cast members, picks up trash.

Other requirements are designed to make the workplace more friendly and pleasant for guests and cast members alike.

Everyone wears a name badge. In many areas, their home city, if it's not local, is printed underneath their name. This provides an opportunity for first-name interaction, and a common ground when they encounter someone whom lives in or knows their hometown.

Everyone is on a first name basis. When camera effects artist Bob Broughton was a new employee at the studio, he was told, "If you bump into Walt, you should say, 'Hi Walt.'" Soon, he was walking down a hallway, and saw Walt Disney approaching. Bob said, "Hi Walt," and Walt walked on by with no reaction.

Bob was embarrassed. "Some minutes later," he said, "I'm coming down this same hall and here comes Walt again. So, this time I walked right by him. And just as I went by, he grabbed me by the arm and says, 'What's the matter? Aren't we speaking?'"[11]

The first name policy is equally true today. I asked a cast member in Tomorrowland, "If you see Disneyland president, Cynthia Harriss, in the park today will you call her by her first name?"

"Absolutely," she said, "I would call her Cynthia."

"What about Michael Eisner?" I asked, referring to Disney's CEO.

"Umm, I'm not sure," she answered honestly. "I've never seen him here, but I'd call him Michael if others were."

Disney has demanding standards of appearance, grooming. Beards are not allowed. Shirts must be tucked in. Costumes and name tags are worn when "on stage."

Moustaches were prohibited for a time, then approved. This illustrates a small degree of flexibility; while the rule was strict, they regularly review these rules and revise them to meet the needs and fashion of the times, while still creating the desired "Disney image."

Cast members are advised:

- Always make eye contact with the customer.

- Never slouch or slump when you're onstage.

- Pointing out something to a guest, use your whole hand, never a single finger. (In some cultures, pointing with a single finger is rude.)

The company sponsors trivia contests for cast members, complete with prizes and award celebrations. This serves to enhance knowledge and pride in the company.

At Disneyland, park anniversaries are subject to celebration. Special pins are designed for cast members to wear on July 17th. Sometimes birthday cake is provided.

Perhaps more than most companies, Disney strives to create a common impression on guests. And the standards are high.

Cast members are trained to treat each other as if they are guests.

The cast members get the big picture.

Leadership

The big picture is, as Walt called it, "the whole package." It encompasses the entire guest experience, from the first call for a reservation or for resort information, until the guest boards the airplane for the trip home.

The big picture also encompasses the entire cast member experience, from the first visit to apply for a job, to coming to work and returning home every day.

None of this would work without complete "buy-in" at the top of the organization. This is where grandiose ideas at other companies often fail; the leaders give lip service to the ideas but fail to follow through like they expect the rest of the staff to do.

At Disney, it works because it starts with the lead managers. There can be no mixed messages; the leader must do what's expected of the rest, because everyone watches.

That's why even senior executives will be seen picking up trash, or straightening a trash receptacle, even though a large group of cast members is hired for that function. Because when front line cast members see it, they know it's expected and it's part of the overall goal. They all pick up trash because it's part of the big picture. It's part of the dream.

It Includes Everything

Disney's corporate culture is designed to cover all the e.
of cast members and guests.

1. It's by design, well thought out.
2. It's well defined, portrayed consistently.
3. It's clear to all. No one has to guess the right thing to do.

Would You Want to Work at Disney?

After reading about all these requirements, you might wonder
if Disney is a pleasant place to work. With the long park hours, job
shifts are often at odd times. Likely shifts would include weekends
and holidays. Clearly it's not right for everyone.

But I found cast members who started at Disneyland during
college, and are still there years later. They love the job. I've visited
with people who joined Disneyland when the park first opened, and
were still there 40 years later. They loved it so much they encouraged
their children to work there, too.

On a recent visit I met cast members who had been at Disneyland
seven years, 20 years, 28 years, 29 years, and one who had been
there 47 years.

Others who had worked at Disneyland, but left, said it was one
of the best experiences of their lives. They said that what they learned
at Disney had helped them in later careers.

How Does This Apply to You Personally?

Think about the culture you've established for yourself and your
family, and the personal culture you've adopted at work.

Write out a list of the things you do, the behaviors you exhibit,
and where you invest your time. What are your skills, your values
and your priorities? Write all that down. Go back through the
corporate list in this chapter and cover similar subjects at the
personal level.

Now go back through the list you just made, and mark the
changes you think would be important to live your life in the best,
finest way possible.

Do you clean up the trash? How can you expect others in the
family or at your job to do so? Do you keep the car clean? Do you
keep the dishes done? Do you value communication with the others
in your life?

How to Use this in Your Company

What is your company culture? What are your roots? Is there a special language that should be in place to help your company's employees work better with internal and external customers?

Think about the culture you've established for your company. Write out a list of the things you do, the behaviors you and your people exhibit, and where time is invested. What are your company's skills, values and priorities? Write all that down. Go back through the list in this chapter and cover similar subjects for your firm.

Now go back through the list you just made, and mark the changes you think would be important to create your company in the best, finest way possible.

Corporate culture is not about the words you write as you make your list, it is about the actual behaviors you and your people exhibit. By writing it all down, you get a handle on what's happening and what you want it to be, and you can begin to grow your culture the way you want it.

Do you personally pick up trash when you come across it, or do you leave it for the janitorial staff? How can you expect others in the company to contribute if you don't do it at every opportunity?

How do you design, define and communicate your company culture to your workforce?

The Culture Becomes a Business Operating Plan

EXECUTION is everything. It's nice to have an idea about what the corporate culture should be, but it has to go beyond the idea. It has to be communicated to everyone, and it has to be made reasonably easy to accomplish within the structure of daily work.

Disney theme parks are known for excellent customer service; they may be the best major company in the world in this regard. What about the rest of the operation? After all, a company is more than customer service, isn't it?

At Disney, it's *all* defined according to service. Shortly after Disneyland opened, Walt made an important change. The security staff was a contracted security force, and the parking lot was run as a concession. Walt quickly came to realize that he needed control of these operations because they, too, came in contact with guests, so the company cancelled those contracts.

Even "backstage" cast members are trained and treated as if they're going to deal with guests. And, occasionally, they do. Overnight cleanup crews may encounter guests leaving the park; they are prepared to assist a guest if needed. The company realized that it could be the last contact the company has with guests before they leave. When guests forget where they parked, parking lot workers are ready to help. Laundry and kitchen workers are taken to onstage areas occasionally so they can see how their work is received. Backstage cast members who may be painting part of an attraction know that their work will enhance a guest's experience.

It's all about service.

In the last chapter we explored how Disney has established a complete Service Plan to run their business. Remember, Disney's Service Theme is, "We create *happiness* by providing *the finest in entertainment* for *people of all ages, everywhere.*"

Service Standards

Within the Service Theme and with a complete understanding of who the guests are and what will create an outstanding experience for them, Disney creates their products and services. They set Service Standards.

In the theme parks, their Service Standards fit four areas:

1. Safety. The first standard, safety, is never sacrificed.

2. Courtesy. Courteous attention to guests provides a good experience.

3. Show. The "show" is the message that guests see and hear while in the park and then take home.

4. Efficiency. Equipment and people must be efficiently deployed to deliver the service and to do so at a fair profit.

Within each of these four areas, Disney establishes definitions and standards for the park and for each attraction.

From the standards, Delivery Systems are developed to deliver on the Service Theme and Service Standards.

Delivery Systems

Delivery of the service and product is actually accomplished by the Delivery Systems, established in three areas:

1. Cast. The employees create and deliver the entertainment, so attention must be given to the process of how they function and how they are treated so that this continues positively over time. This includes hiring, training, rehearsing, and taking care of the employees.

2. Setting. The setting is defined as "onstage," or anywhere that there is customer contact. The setting is a delivery system, too, as it is part of the show. Whether it's accessing an internet website, waiting in line to buy tickets, sitting down to eat, or using a rest room, the setting affects the guest. It's part of the show.

3. Operating Systems. Additional operating systems are also part of the delivery. This includes systems for scheduling, reservations, purchasing, and receiving, plus utilities, banking, and staffing.

Process Integration

When it's all operating correctly, the systems work together smoothly and guests don't even realize what's happening. The goal is to satisfy guests every day in outstanding ways.

I stopped by a cart in Fantasyland where small toys were being sold. Two cast members were present; one was holding a clipboard with a computer printout. I asked her about it; she said she was a manager and was checking the work schedule to make sure everything was staffed and working like it was supposed to.

It seemed like pretty standard management, but as I thought about it I realized that I'd not seen anyone with a computer printout in Fantasyland before. Computer printouts don't fit in Fantasyland, so they're usually kept well hidden.

Most of the time, when you visit with a cast member they're just visiting with you. Unless you've asked for schedule information, it's pure person-to-person. At least, it seems that way.

In fact, Disney has mastered the integration of systems so front line cast members usually can concentrate on guests without tending to computer printouts.

Disney has established systems to make it possible for the culture to work in the company, including a number of communications methods, hiring procedures, training strategies, and ongoing cast support programs.

It also has to be maintained, so no one forgets what it's all about, and it may have to be adjusted to meet the changing realities of a changing world.[12]

How Does This Apply to You Personally?

What is important to you? Do you organize your time so you focus on the important, rather than on the urgent?

Do you maintain a family calendar, posted where everyone can see it to stay organized? Do you have a personal calendar and planner? Do you keep notes organized in a binder, and in files, or are scraps of paper constantly being misplaced?

Do you make a daily "Things to Do" list, and use it each day to stay focused and accomplish more?

Do you have a place to put bills that need to be paid, a day and time for paying bills, and a place to file them when you're done so you can find your records when you need them?

What systems can you put in place to make your life follow the plan you have just laid out?

How to Use this in Your Company

I've watched other firms, unrelated to Disney, try to adopt certain Disney strategies and fail. An electronics and appliance chain, Incredible Universe, called employees "cast members," and customers "guests." When they were on the retail sales floor they were "on stage." And the stores failed. Why? First, they didn't have a show business background, like Disney, so the language made no sense. Their culture was not communicated well, and their staff did not "buy in" to what they were doing. The "host-guest" language was appropriate but the show business lingo was not. The employees didn't get it, and neither did the customers.

The "show" they created was unlike Disney and lacked broad appeal. They tried to use the *concept,* without creating the appropriate *culture* and service theme. You can do better.

What is your Service Theme? Can you look at Disney's and modify it to fit your business? Fill in the blanks for the four key elements: "We create *(what emotion)* by providing *(what product or service)* for *(whom, and for what geographic or other location)*."

What about your Service Standards? Disney has established standards in Safety, Show, Courtesy, and Efficiency. What would your four or five areas be? How will you define them? What are the specific areas and guidelines within each?

Can you now look at operating procedures and processes that meet those standards and deliver on the Service Theme? Can you address these processes in terms of Staff, Setting, and other Delivery Systems?

In the process, you may find a number of easy, inexpensive ways to build a more positive culture.

The Discovery that Makes Disney Park Attractions Unique

A COMPELLING STORY is part of each ride, and that's an important part of Disney's theme park magic. Walt wanted everyone who came to Disneyland to leave an attraction smiling. He knew he had to make a ride fun, and the best way to do that was to let the guest experience a story.

Walt was a marvelous story teller, and infused enthusiasm to his audience. A major part of Walt's success with cartoons was his ability to create cartoons with a good story line.

In the early studio days, animators had a difficult time explaining their concepts and developing story lines in what was a mostly visual medium. Words just didn't convey the story in a way that they could effectively plot and plan a cartoon. They would bring sketches to a story session but the continuity of what would appear on the screen was difficult to imagine and even more difficult to remember.

A solution was developed. Walt said it was invented by animator Webb Smith, who started pinning sketches to the wall. As the story was changed, sketches could be added or moved, depicting the new structure.

It was effective, but distressed Walt because the process was tearing up the newly redecorated walls. So he ordered large fiber boards, four by eight feet, which could be placed horizontally on easels.[13] Suddenly the "storyboard" had been created. Using a moveable board was particularly handy, because a series of boards could be placed along a wall for a story session, and moved out of the way for other boards for artists working on other projects.

The basic concept for a storyboard was not really new; it was used by Leonardo da Vinci to sequence his ideas. But the implementation was new, and Disney used it well.

The storyboard looks something like a comic strip on a bulletin board. It also looks something like a scheduling board in an office, or maybe even your home refrigerator, covered with papers and cards.

Personal Interaction

The storyboards became central tools for development of story lines. Walt would join animators for story sessions, and act out various scenes the way he envisioned them. Artists would suggest characters, actions, or dialogue. Quick sketches would be placed on the boards and the story would take shape.

Story sessions became brainstorming and planning sessions, and the storyboards made it possible to track the process. Often a stenographer was also present to record and type up the discussion. Walt had created a "brain trust" with himself and his animators, and it was extremely productive.

Soon the storyboard method was adopted by other studios and applied to live action as well as animation. Today it continues to be used, and has even been adopted by advertising agencies creating television commercials.

Storyboards are used to plan, get ideas, communicate, and organize.

A Planning Secret for Disney Theme Parks

Walt was using the storyboard as a central tool in all kinds of business discussions. He found it useful, yet he probably started using it outside the animation process simply because it was how he was used to working.

So, when it was time to plan attractions for Disneyland, the storyboard system was used.

As a management and planning tool, the storyboard session was powerful. Combined with Walt's experience developing stories for animation, Disneyland planning created effective "stories" for rides. This was a major departure from typical amusement park planning, and the story added immensely to the guest's experience at an attraction.

Other parks in the intervening years have tried to duplicate Disneyland's success; one of the major difficulties is their failure to storyboard the ride effectively and create a compelling story for the attraction.

By the time the Disney company was developing the Florida project, the storyboard process had evolved into an effective management tool. As a result the company created the plans for Disney World in Florida in just ten days.

Make Storyboarding Work for You

Storyboarding assists in problem solving and is especially effective creating and deciding on alternatives.

Writing a list of ideas on a flip chart during a meeting is *not* storyboarding. While flip charts may facilitate a visual review of ideas generated, and even empower those in a group to build on each other's ideas, the flip chart lacks the flexibility of having each idea on a separate card so cards can be repositioned to form new solutions.

Traditional brainstorming may be effective on narrowly defined problems. Storyboarding is much more effective, and may be expected to produce two to three times as many ideas. Storyboarding is useful for solving complex problems, and can be carried further into the project execution stage.

I first learned about storyboarding in the late 70's from Mike Vance, who was in charge of idea and people development for Disney fifteen years earlier when Walt Disney World was being planned. Mike helped Disney take storyboarding to a new level, and he has been influential in taking the concept outside Disney. If you've ever used any of these techniques, perhaps by another name, it's probably because of the efforts of Mike Vance to teach it to corporate America.

Next time you have a complex problem to solve or a project to organize, take your thoughts and those of others and put them on index cards. Then spread them out on a storyboard. Reorganize them into logical groups and prioritize them. You'll begin to see interconnections, how ideas relate, and how the pieces fit together.

At Home and in the Workplace

Storyboarding is useful both at work and at home. It can be used to facilitate a group planning session, or can be used by an individual to enhance their insight and grasp of a problem or project.

Where should you do your storyboard?

At home, you can buy a big bulletin board and hang it on the wall. Go to the discount store, the stationery store, or the drug store and buy a pack of index cards, and some masking tape or push pins. Or, find a clear wall and dedicate that space to storyboarding. If that's not practical, you can clear off the dinner table, or clear off the bed, and use that flat surface to spread out index cards, papers, and drawings.

At work, you can hang large bulletin boards, or find clear wall space for storyboarding. As you discover the success of the process, redecorate meeting rooms so entire walls can be used for storyboarding, with easy visual and direct access to the walls.

In the early years, Disney used four by eight foot fiber boards, and would put them on easels. Later, rooms with high ceilings were used for storyboarding, and the fiber boards could be hung on the walls. Even hallways were equipped to hang storyboards.

Today, "white boards" are popular in meeting rooms, but they're difficult to use for storyboarding. It's difficult to erase a section and rewrite it; for a storyboard you want to be able to pick up a card and move it to a new location quickly.

If you use push pins to hold your cards to the board, you'll need a bulletin board or fiber board. If you use masking tape, nearly any kind of board or wall will do. Using boards affords portability and creates a sort of "infinite wall."

Artistic Talent Not Required

Do you have to be an artist to make storyboarding work? No! In fact, you don't even have to draw any pictures! You're probably not planning a *Snow White* or a *Pirates of the Caribbean*. Those might require drawings and art. For most business applications, you can use a combination of 5x8 and 3x5 index cards. You'll be writing words on the cards, or occasionally a diagram or symbol, if it's easier.

It's important that everyone participate, so someone has to be in charge and make sure no one is left out. It's always helpful to do something in the beginning to relax the group so ideas are not inhibited. And, it's important to encourage participation by each person.

Walt acted as facilitator in those early Disney story sessions; eventually others led storyboard sessions.

Once ideas start flowing, everyone will become involved in the process. They will begin to add to or embellish each other's ideas.

The specific process is simple:

1. Problem. Agree on a topic. Identify the problem or project. Describe the current situation. Establish the purpose.

2. Possibilities. Seek suggestions for possible causes, then for possible solutions. Various possibilities are suggested. As with brainstorming, each person's suggestions rate equally. Each is written on a card and posted to the board. This encourages everyone to contribute freely.

3. Grouping. The cards are grouped so related cards are together. Then groups are placed in a logical order.

4. Priorities. Each group is sorted by priority.

5. Re-Ordering. Examine resources and restraints. Cards are re-ordered to make logical sense and to eliminate duplication of ideas. Select a solution. The result is discussed and revised as required.

Throughout the process, it is the group interaction that creates a sum greater than the combination of the parts. Ideas grow as they are reflected off others in the group. Storylines develop. Solutions are presented.

The storyboard may be photographed or left in place for reference and for further planning sessions.

Four Kinds of Storyboards

There are four kinds of storyboards commonly used to solve complex problems in business. Each serves a specific purpose. Less complex problems may be handled on a single storyboard.

The primary boards are the Planning Storyboard, used to analyze a problem and generate solutions, and the Ideas Storyboard, used to expand on the key ideas and refine a specific solution. The two boards work together to define a problem, to generate available solutions, and to expand and develop the best ideas.

Two additional boards are the Project Briefing Storyboard and the Communication Storyboard. These are used only if needed.

Look at how each storyboard is used:

1. Planning Storyboard. The first step in the storyboard process, the Planning Board creates a blueprint for solving the problem in question.

The Planning Board is set up with a Project Description card on the top, and below it goes a row of header cards. A header card, labeled *Purpose,* is placed on the left side of the header row, and on the right side another header card labeled *Misc.*

The first step working with the Planning Board is to agree on the problem (the Project Description), and establish the purpose of the project. As you and the group start brainstorming, put all ideas on the board.

With that done, assemble the cards into related groups. The result should be a natural grouping of ideas, which you can then consolidate and write new cards, as needed, to reflect the new idea. Each group should be placed under a new heading.

Now do a grouping on all the Purpose cards, and prioritize these so you have four or five main points.

Proceed to the other heading groupings, and brainstorm each heading to expand the ideas. Then group, prioritize, and reorder to organize the heading.

Work through each of the headings in this manner.

Any time you're in doubt, look back at the cards under the Purpose heading, and evaluate what to include or disregard.

2. **Ideas Storyboard.** The Ideas Board is an expansion of related ideas contained in the Planning Board.

In the Planning Board session, certain ideas may be dropped. Others need to be developed further, and the Ideas Board is used for that purpose.

Related headers are copied to the Ideas board, and the brainstorming begins. During this session, additional headers may get created, and ideas added to both new and existing headers.

Then cards are grouped, prioritized, and reordered, until the idea is developed and planned.

3. **Project Briefing Storyboard.** This board, sometimes called an Organization Board, is used to take the plans from the Planning and Ideas boards and organizes them into individual and group objectives and tasks. It then serves as a project status update (a "briefing") for anyone who needs to know where things stand..

This board is typically set up with three main headers, *Do,* where you would post tasks that need to be done, *Doing,* where you post tasks that are underway, and *Done* where you post completed tasks. As the project is underway, task cards are moved from Do, to Doing, to Done.

Two other headers would be *Holdups,* where you would post a card for anything that was holding up the project where help is needed, and *Inputs,* where people can leave you notes with suggestions for handling the holdups.

4. **Communication Storyboard.** When a number of people outside the project need to know about the project and its progress, a Communication board can be used to organize communications. On it you would organize who needs to know, what they need to know, when they need to know it, and how the communication will be done.

Great things happen in a group when everyone's having fun. Walt would act out portions of a story, and quick drawings and idea notes would be put on the storyboard. Others would contribute ideas, and the story would grow. These were relaxed, but high energy sessions; as the story took form the excitement grew. And everyone then knew what needed to be done.

Always Promoting, Cross Promoting

"Gags" were the key to early cartoons, but soon Walt needed more than gags. Walt Disney was always a promoter. He exploited new technology, adding sound and later full color to cartoons, aware that these things would create a stir and bring out the public.

It probably started in Kansas City. As an employee of Kansas City Film Ad Company, and then at Walt's own Laugh-O-Gram Films, he made short movies – today we would call them commercials – for local companies to be shown at the theaters.

When television first started developing in the 30's Walt's attitude was the same as other movie producers; they weren't interested, fearing the new technology would hurt the movie business.

Television networks pursued Walt, and by the early 50's he produced a couple of specials.

Still, he remained pretty negative toward television until one morning when he awakened with the idea that television might be used to finance Disneyland. He was able to hold the "carrot" for a network, offering to produce television programs, and in return he wanted normal payment plus investment in Disneyland. ABC bought the idea.

It was a brilliant strategy, especially when he decided one of those programs would be a *Disneyland* television show, each week on a different subject. The show debuted nearly a year before the opening of Disneyland Park, with Walt himself as host.

The first week's program was all about what was being built in Anaheim, blatantly an hour-long commercial for Disney, broken up with paid commercials from sponsors. Critics were outraged, but viewers didn't seem to mind; they lapped it up. And the network didn't mind; after all, they owned 35 per cent of the park!

The show quickly became the first program on ABC to get into the top 20 Nielsen ratings. Disney combined new production with old footage to create programs, at one point creating a program about making the movie *20,000 Leagues Under the Sea;* the result was another long promotional program. He frequently did hour-long features about the park.

By the time Disneyland opened, additional coverage on the television program, combined with the efforts of the studio's experienced public relations department, resulted in millions of people who were itching to visit the park.

Many of the early attractions at Disneyland were tied in to Disney movies, cartoons, and television shows: Peter Pan Flight *(Peter Pan)*, Mad Tea Party *(Alice in Wonderland)*, Snow White's Adventures *(Snow White)*, Mike Fink Keel Boats *(Davy Crockett)*, Jungle Cruise *(True-Life Adventures)*, Casey Jr. Circus Train *(Casey, Jr.)*, Dumbo Flying Elephants *(Dumbo)*, Rocket to the Moon *(Man in Space)*, and Mickey Mouse Club Theater *(Mickey Mouse Club)*.

The castle, more a Disneyland landmark than an attraction, was first referred to as "The Medieval Castle." Later, in an early *Disneyland* TV show, Walt Disney called it "Snow White's Castle." During park construction, it was known as "Fantasyland Castle." By opening day, it was renamed "Sleeping Beauty Castle," anticipating Disney's release of that movie four years later.

This illustrates the value Disney placed on cross-promotion. Park visitors see the castle, and it promotes the new movie. The movie promotes the castle. And the television program ties it all together, making sure the promotional value is realized.

Movie promotion, television, and audience response: Disneyland served to consolidate the Disney enterprise.

Today, the studio has started to reverse the idea. Attractions with no linked film have had films created for them, i.e., movies titled *The Haunted Mansion* and *Pirates of the Caribbean*.

Merchandising

Promotion doesn't stop with movies and television. Music is marketed as CDs, cassettes, and sheet music. Books, comic books, and newspaper comic strips are produced. Products are created to tie in to movies and attractions.

Worldwide product sales create tremendous royalty income for Disney, and there are even bigger profits when products are sold in the park and the company realizes the retail margin.

The overall value extends far beyond royalties and retail profits.

Think of the emotional connection created when a youngster adopts his or her favorite plush toy, and it's a Disney character. That connection will result in purchases and loyalty to Disney lines, perhaps even through several generations. Later releases of sequels in theaters or home video are more readily accepted, and the cycle repeats.

Roy Disney said, "Integration is the key word around here; we don't do anything in one line without giving a thought to its likely profitability in other lines."[14]

Walt said, "I'm not Disney anymore. I used to be Disney, but now Disney is something we've built up in the public mind over the years. It stands for something, and you don't have to explain what it is to the public."[15]

How You Can Use Self-Promotion Effectively

As children we're often taught humility, and we're taught that it's rude to be a braggart. For our own protection, we're taught not to talk to strangers. As adults, this may work against our self-interest.

When it comes to getting a job, earning a promotion, persuading someone to an important decision, or selling an idea at a meeting, you'll shine if you use the magic of self-promotion.

Disney built his name and reputation into something respected. It gave him influence and power. You can do the same thing on a personal scale.

You want your family, your employer, your fellow workers, and your customers to know what you stand for, and to respect your opinions and offerings. To establish that, you need to promote. I'm not suggesting rudeness; I am suggesting that you be known.

There are two elements to successful personal promotion: Your network and your outreach activities.

Your Personal List

Start today to collect the names, addresses, phone numbers and email addresses of everyone you can. Keep them in a personal address book, or on your home computer (and be sure to back up the data and print it out regularly).

Collect names of your family, your friends, people you meet at parties and meetings, people you go to school or classes with, people you meet at religious and community gatherings, your coworkers, your bosses, vendors you use at home and at work, customers you know, and anyone else who comes to mind.

Jot down additional information when you can get it, like birthdays, spouse names, and children's names.

Frankly, we should be taught to start this when we're about 12 years old, and keep collecting names the rest of our lives. Since you're probably older than 12, the good news is that it's never too late to start. If you have children, teach them this; as they get older knowing how to reach their old friends will be valuable.

Home addresses are best, but do what you can. Get both home and work if you can, where appropriate. For students at college be sure to get home addresses so mail can reach them when the term is over.

It would be a good idea to keep your list current and maintain at least minimum contact with everyone. Mail a holiday greeting card or holiday letter once a year to everyone on your list.

Under your return address at the top left corner of the front of your envelope, write "Return Service Requested." That tells the post office that if someone moves, not to forward the card. Instead, if they have a new address they'll put it on the envelope and return it to you so you can update your address book. And if there is no forwarding address, you'll learn that, too.

This way you'll keep your list up to date for years, even though most people won't write to tell you their new address.

Now you have a promotion database, a list of people who you can keep informed about what good things are happening in your life.

You also have a resource list that you can use when you, or anyone you know, needs to find a vendor or someone with special skills or contacts.

Your Outreach Activities

Now let's look at your outreach activities. The key here is that you don't want to be a wallflower. Staying hidden will defeat you.

A close friend of mine is an administrative assistant at a big company. She told me the other day she enjoyed her company's holiday party so much, she wanted to send the CEO and the president thank you letters. But she was having second thoughts. "I don't want to draw attention to myself," she said.

"Yes, you do!" I almost shouted. "That's exactly what you want to do. Forget all those things you learned as a child about being humble. You want to let them know who you are. Find any excuse you can to send them a note, or to forward them some information you think they should have.

"When you find a newspaper or magazine article you think they should see, send them a copy. It's okay if you think they probably have seen the article already. Maybe they didn't, and if they have, they'll know you're in tune with the company's goals."

It's also a good idea to do things to make a personal impression. Learn to speak up at meetings, send thank you notes and positive suggestions at every opportunity, and ask others for their suggestions when you're trying to accomplish something.

Think about cross-promotion. Tell your friends, your coworkers, and your boss about things you can do to help in addition to the main activity they associate with you.

Don't just do it. *Tell them.*

Your Personal Booster Club

From your list of contacts identify about two dozen who have a good idea of what you stand for and what you're trying to do with your life.

Just about everyone has a group of people who are willing to encourage them and "champion" them to other people. These will be people who are in a position to impact your business or career.

Once you've identified them, make a plan to contact each of them monthly in some way, by a phone call, a letter, a fax, a postcard, or a personal visit. You can send them an interesting article you've clipped from a newspaper or magazine, or give them a three sentence report on how things are going for you.

These people become a personal "boosters club," a group of people you can rely on to help promote you and your causes, just as you would help them.

You Can Expand Promotion in Your Company

If you're running a company, or in management, think about the opportunities you have for expanding promotion.

Remember what Roy Disney said: "We don't do anything in one line without giving a thought to its likely profitability in other lines."

What other products can you sell that relate to existing products, so that selling one will lead to selling the other? Can you bundle related items so you sell several things instead of one? If you sell a service item, what can you package with your service so it promotes a product?

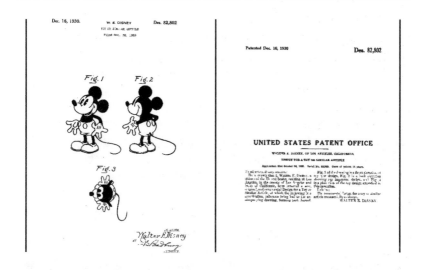

Recognizing the value of cross-line promotion, Disney filed for a patent for a Mickey Mouse toy Oct. 30, 1929, approximately one year after Mickey's introduction in *Steamboat Willie*. This patent was awarded Dec. 16, 1930.

Disneyland: Never Finished

MYSTERY WAS WAITING in Tomorrowland. It was 1986, my first visit to Disneyland, and I was already loving it. A section of Tomorrowland was boarded up. Something new was under construction. It was called "Star Tours."

I was so overwhelmed by Disneyland at that moment that the significance of Star Tours didn't register until several visits later.

When Star Tours finally opened in 1987, the lines were really long. Now, I don't mean long in the sense that it always seems like the lines are long. These lines wound around Tomorrowland and extended south into Main Street, U.S.A.

Clearly, Star Tours was a big hit.

Two years later, "Splash Mountain" opened.

Three years after that, "Fantasmic!" was introduced.

Two more years and "Roger Rabbit's Car Toon Spin" opened, followed the next year by "Indiana Jones Adventure - The Temple of the Forbidden Eye."

It took me 31 years to get to Disneyland the first time, and they were still building it!

Walt Disney said, "If there's something I don't like at Disneyland, I can correct it. I can always change it [in the park], but not in the films."

The lesson was clear: Being able to make changes at Disneyland allows the park to grow and entertain more visitors. It keeps the park up-to-date with technology. It allows attractions to improve and entertain better.

Over time, I began to see smaller changes that enhanced the Disneyland experience.

An information center appeared in the center of Disneyland, displaying the current wait times for each attraction. With this information, a guest can choose an attraction with a shorter wait, and crowds are diverted to better utilize the facilities.

Regular refurbishment of all attractions provides for major maintenance and changes, some so slight you might not be certain they occurred.

Last time I rode Pirates of the Caribbean, the lighting was changed on one scene, there was a new character interaction, and the sound track was changed slightly. I think. There's so much detail in Disney attractions, you can still discover new things on the 100th ride, even if no changes were made!

Holiday decorations brighten up the park at holidays, and certain attractions are changed for the holidays. A special holiday parade is staged.

The computerized *FastPass* system was implemented to let guests get a "reservation" time for an attraction. This lets guests avoid standing in the long lines, and during that time guests can shop, eat, or enjoy another ride.

Walt said, "The park means a lot to me. It's something that will never be finished, something I can keep developing, keep 'plussing,' and adding to. It's alive. It will be a live, breathing thing that will need changes... not only can I add things to it, but even the trees will keep growing. The thing will get more beautiful year after year. And it will get better as I find out what the public likes."[16]

How to Use this at Home

It's an interesting paradox of life; people thrive on change, yet they resist it.

Think for a moment about how your life has changed over the years. Major changes are changing schools, changing jobs, and moving to new homes.

Lifestyle changes include moving from school to the workplace, getting married, having children, and losing a spouse to death or divorce.

Other changes may be things you've initiated, like redecorating a room, or your home. Or buying a different car. Or meeting new friends, joining a new club, watching a new television show, or visiting a new restaurant.

Sometimes just changing your daily routine or the way you interact with your spouse or your best friend will charge your life with new enthusiasm.

My wife, Sharon, and I go for a neighborhood walk early most mornings. When we take the time to look for and see different things along that path, or to divert and take a different path, it opens our day to new adventure.

At Disneyland, it takes a combination of big and small changes to keep things interesting.

What in your life can you change to make it more interesting for you and those around you? What can you change to do things better, or for lower cost, or faster and with less effort? The changes don't have to be big; they can be small, even subtle.

Make a list. Put that list in a prominent place where you will see it daily, to make positive change part of your life.

How to Use this at Work

Sharon likes to change her job every couple of years. That doesn't mean she changes employers, it simply means she has to take on new responsibilities, or change the way she's doing things, in order to avoid boredom.

We each have a different threshold for boredom, a different attention span. Introducing change can serve a number of different purposes.

What can you change in your workplace to make work more interesting? More fun?

Is there something you can change to make the work easier, or faster? Can you make it better? Can you do it for less money? Can you make it more useful?

What if you work on a production line and they won't let you change anything? Do you whistle or hum a song while you work? Try it. Or imagine it. Change the song. Imagine the people who will ultimately use the product you build. How will they be using it? How do they spend their days? Where do they go on vacation? What do they do that you would never do? What do you do that they will never do?

Even changing the subjects you think about will introduce change to your job, make it more interesting, and, hopefully, more fun.

How to Use this in Your Company

My friend, Paul Brown, used to run a restaurant. Every spring, he would have the restaurant repainted with a fresh coat of paint. Then he would start changing the menu, adding new items, hoping to interest more customers, or more repeat business.

Quite some years ago, McDonald's realized that their facilities were unused in the mornings, and their customers were eating breakfast elsewhere. So they added breakfast sandwiches, and hot cakes, and expanded the business with relatively little cost.

What can you change about your business to get the work done faster, or better, or for lower cost?

What can you do within your business to serve your customers better, to make them want more of your products or services, or to purchase from you more often?

What can you do to make your business new for your customers, so that each time they come back they can enjoy the experience in a new way, even if it is a subtle difference?

How Disney Uses Attention to Detail to Create Magic

FROGS. FIREFLIES. LILY PADS. Prior to 1967, if I asked you to think of the environment around a pirate's cave, those items probably would have missed your list.

Instead, you'd have told me about pieces of eight, skeletons, pirate hats, sunken ships, and buried treasure.

Then, *Pirates of the Caribbean* opened in New Orleans Square at Disneyland. The first effect is a quiet evening in the bayou, complete with frogs croaking, fireflies winking, and an old guy playing a mouth harp, sitting on the porch of his shack at the edge of that sluggish stream that meanders through the lowlands.

Walt was insistent that the attractions relate a story, and that the guest experience was complete only if the story was well told. One major Disney magic secret is attention to detail. The frogs and fireflies are examples of that detail.

First Impressions

When you first enter Disneyland, you find the railroad, with two tunnels under the track. Those tunnels lead to Main Street U.S.A.

Walt wanted to hang curtains in the tunnels, so, just like at a theater, every visitor would see the curtains open, and the show taking place beyond. Visitors would step through and become part of the show!

His planners convinced him that with the thousands of people who would be at Disneyland every day, the curtain opening was impractical. Still, by moving through that short tunnel, a guest gets the feeling of walking into a new, different, storybook world.

One detail that makes it possible is the "berm," the raised earthen platform for the railroad. It encloses the entire park, blocking out the outside world and giving Disney control of what you see and hear.

By paying attention to details, they tap the crowd's psychology in the park.

Large visual attractions in each area of the park are designed to draw traffic patterns in specific directions. When you enter Main Street U.S.A., you see the castle at the far end. It pulls you through Main Street to the "hub."

At the hub, you'll see the futuristic action in Tomorrowland to one side, and the Steamboat in Frontierland opposite. And the castle will still be pulling you to walk through.

Walt's planners learned that crowds tend to turn right, rather than left, so as you leave Main Street, the path into Tomorrowland is wider than the paths on the left into Adventureland and Frontierland.

Walt didn't want guests to go into a pretend area, like other parks. He wanted it to be a storybook, so he told his planners to make everything five-eighths size. So, Main Street, the castle, New Orleans Square... everything is built with a forced storybook perspective. Since guests would be entering the main floor of buildings, the first floor facade is designed at 90 percent of normal. (A four-foot high doorway wouldn't have worked.) Second floors are designed at eighty per cent, and third floors at sixty per cent.

They even had bricks and materials made in proportional sizes to ensure the illusion.

The result is more than a feeling that you've walked into a miniature storybook world. As you walk among the buildings and look up, the forced perspective suggests taller buildings. The result is a bit unreal, and contributes to the fantasy.

The train was built to five-eighths scale, with a bit of extra room for the engineer up front. The steamboat, too, was built as a miniature of a full-sized steamboat, but adapted for passengers. The result? When you climb aboard, you feel like you've walked into a childlike storybook world. Everything seems full size, but it's not.

Something New

Walt knew the details help create the right mood.

When you arrive in the morning, you'll likely find the Disneyland band playing light and happy music. In the afternoon the band retires and jazz combos appear in New Orleans Square. By evening, the music slows down a bit to match the mood of the crowd.

Walt also knew that many of the guests would be returning again and again. He said that if there was enough detail, folks would see something new every time they came, as they noticed things they missed before.

So even tiny details are created and maintained.

The gold color on the King Arthur Carousel is real gold leaf, not gold paint.

The pretend signs and names on Main Street U.S.A. (and in other areas of the park) name key people from the planning and history of the park. "Elias Disney, Contractor," on a Main Street window pays homage to Walt's dad, who really was a construction contractor much of his adult life.

You'll find things like a $50,000 chandelier hanging in a restaurant, because Walt felt that it might make you feel better eating there, even if you didn't know what it cost.

The walkways in Frontierland are made of concrete, but it's tinted brown and poured uneven to look and feel like walking on hardened mud. If you look closely, you'll see boot prints, horseshoe impressions, and buggy tracks, just like you might expect in an old western town. These details aren't required, but they enhance the impression.

Two weeks after it opened, I walked through the California Adventure park. The walkways in the Condor Flats area were cracked and chipped, as if it was an old desert road. Freshly planted palm trees were untrimmed and distressed, with long brown fronds drooping toward the ground. This is quite a contrast to the normal Disney approach with beautiful streets and landscaping, but it was needed to create the image.

Hidden Mickeys

It's been a custom in show business for many years to hide images or messages in set designs, costumes, and even dialog. It's a sort of inside joke; the audience won't get it, but the insider will. That idea was carried into Disneyland and other Disney theme parks.

Designers tantalize diehard Disney fans by hiding images of Mickey Mouse, usually circles depicting his head and ears, in décor and architecture, creating a puzzle of images to find on their next visit. Some are relatively obvious; many are well hidden. More than just adding detail, it creates puzzles throughout the property, and thousands of people look for them.

In Pirates of the Caribbean, it's been said the main sail of the pirate ship is shaped like Mickey. And some of those lily pads in the opening scene are arranged as a hidden Mickey. I've looked for these, and not been able to see them, but others swear they are there.

In the Haunted Mansion, the second place setting from the right in the dining hall is three plates, set to form a Mickey.

The Grand Californian Hotel has a Mickey, or multiple Mickeys, in every lamp.

In California Adventure's "Soarin' Over California," there's a Mickey on the golf ball that flies by. You have to look quick to catch that one!

When it was built, Disneyland was out in the middle of the orange groves near Anaheim and Walt had some latitude picking Disneyland's address, 1313 Harbor Boulevard. 'M' is the 13th letter in the alphabet, so 1313 is "MM," Mickey Mouse's initials.

Commitment to Quality

Attractions in the park, and the park itself, are designed to "tell a story" by giving an experience that you can't get any other place.

During the construction of New Orleans Square in the early 1960's, Disney ordered the work torn up and restarted because he didn't like the way it was going.

Walt insisted on a genuine commitment to quality. Designers and managers appreciated the insistence that visitors get their money's worth, through a continuous search for new ideas, new angles, and new additions.

Imagineer Marc Davis tells of proposals to rework a park ride, explaining that there was a cheap way to do it and an expensive way. Walt's response? "Marc, you and I do not worry whether anything is cheap or expensive. We only worry whether it's good. I have a theory that if it's good enough, the public will pay you back for it."[17]

You can Use Details to Add Magic to Your Life

There's magic in the details. Think about the difference between a dinner at a typical family eatery, and dinner at a pricey upscale restaurant. The vegetables are the same. It's nearly the same cut of meat. You still have one server who takes your order and brings most of your food.

But the difference is everything. And it's all in the details.

The upscale restaurant makes a "presentation" of the menu, and of the food. The table is carefully set; the china and tableware are nicer. Even the bill is presented in a more elegant way.

So the price is higher, and the tips are bigger. And the experience is hardly comparable.

Attention to the tiny details creates higher quality and a better experience. The Hidden Mickeys? An example of attention to detail, detail that most guests will not even see. But those that do will be intrigued.

What about healthcare? When you go in for an operation, do you want them taking care of all the little details? Or is it okay if they leave a sponge or two inside?

Is it important to ruthlessly keep track of whose baby is whose in the hospital nursery? They all look almost the same.

In these cases, the importance of details is obvious. The details make a big difference where they're not so obvious, too. That was Walt's secret, and it's magic you can use.

What little details can you do at home to make your family's lives better?

What can you do in your company to do the little things that make the big things right?

Guestology, Disney's Link to Customer Service

HUNGRY, we arrived early at Disneyland. Sharon walked quickly with me over to the River Belle restaurant for breakfast. We ordered the Steamboat platter, a combination of eggs, bacon, and pancakes.

This time, we were served on plastic plates. We grumbled a bit because the plates were flimsy and not as nice as the plates they had been using.

That evening, we had dinner at the Carnation Café. When dinner was served, again it was on plastic plates. The server explained it was a new policy.

As we left the park that night we stopped by the Guest Relations office at City Hall, and wrote up a complaint about downgrading the service to plastic throwaway plates. And the next time we visited, the nicer plates had returned.

Was it our complaint? Probably it was ours combined with a number of others, because Disney listens to its customers.

They call it *Guestology;* it's all about knowing their guests.

In other firms, it might be called market research, or consumer research, and it might be left for the marketing department to review at a convenient time.

At Disney, it's personal. They review this input constantly and adjust operations accordingly.

It starts with paying attention to what guests have to say by paying attention to comment cards, letters, and email. And it goes further.

Multiple Methods of Gathering Information

As you walk into a Disney theme park, or as you leave, or as you exit an attraction, you may be greeted by a cast member with a clipboard, or a computer disguised as a clipboard. If you agree, you'll be asked questions ranging from "Where are you staying?" and "Did you like the flowers in the hub area?" to "Please rate the show you just saw on a scale of one to ten," and "What can we do to make your visit more fun?"

Disney learned long ago to formalize information gathering with face-to-face surveys, telephone surveys, and utilization studies, counting what people eat or which attractions they use most.

Telephone surveys after they return home to guests who stayed at Disney hotels harvest information about vacation trends and guest reactions.

Utilization surveys involve counting hamburgers and beef stew sold in the park's restaurants, and counting how many guests choose one attraction over another at various times of the day. This information provides input for menu revisions, cast staffing, and new attraction development.

Listening Posts

Disney also places kiosks and counters at various points in the park, staffed with Guest Relations specialists. In addition to providing guests with information, directions, and schedules, these become "listening posts" where information is gathered.

Perhaps the most important method is the utilization of thousands of cast members throughout the park and at hotels and restaurants nearby. They have first hand knowledge of what's happening, and they have direct contact with guests.

When you have lunch, your server may ask you questions like, "Have you had fun in the park today?" "How were the wait times?" "What would have made the wait better for you?"

They will also note comments you make, like, "The churros aren't hot like they used to be," or, "Why don't they give us something to do while we're sitting on the curb waiting for the parade?"

Comments cover situations right in the cast member's work area, and throughout the park. These are passed to managers right away so problems can be corrected.

If a cast member hears of something urgent, they are encouraged to pass it along right away so it can be fixed.

Another guestology method is focus groups, organized to evaluate park promotions, new attractions, and ideas being formulated for park development.

"Secret shoppers" are used to shop various retail and food areas to check pricing, merchandise arrangement, and guest service. These shoppers create reports which carry a lot of weight with managers in the various areas.

Surveys repeatedly indicate that the three things guests like best are the outstanding "show," the exacting cleanliness, and the friendly employees. This is precisely the list of things Walt wanted to create when he started thinking about Disneyland.

Creative Advisory Council

At Disneyland they have a "Creative Advisory Council," a focus group selected by the Disneyland merchants and consisting of frequent guests, cast members, and even an Imagineer.

They meet about four times a year in Anaheim.

The council is primarily tasked with merchandise development and merchandise related events. But since they meet with resort buyers and top executives, it becomes a powerful tool for input from dedicated guests.

The Guest Compass: N, W, S, and E

Guests are analyzed in four key areas:

1. Needs. Required products or services are the focus of this point on the compass. Basic food, water, and shelter would be examples.

2. Wants. Defined as the things a person wants beyond actual need. This may be an enhanced version of a need. For example, water is a basic need, and bottled water is probably a want. Being able to satisfy wants successfully makes it possible to exceed guest expectations.

3. Stereotypes. This is the image people already have of the company, the industry, and the employees. Where these stereotypes may be negative, the focus becomes overcoming the stereotype. At a Disney theme park, this would be handled through cleanliness, cast member costumes, friendliness, etc.

4. Emotions. Less tangible, and therefore harder to define, emotions are the actual gauge for successful guest service. Emotions must be considered and channeled to satisfactory outcomes.[18]

How to Use Guestology Every Day

Ask family and coworkers what would make their day go better. We're all acquainted with the question, "How are you?" But that is so overused it seldom gathers any truly useful information.

Think about the questions that might elicit good ideas.

"What would make lunchtime more enjoyable?"

"How can we plan our next vacation so everyone has a good time?"

"Can you think of anything that would make it easier for you when I drop off this work?"

Note these are asking for specific information. The questions reflect concern, and elicit ideas. At Disney, guests report they appreciate being asked for specific ideas like, "What would have made the wait more fun?"

Making it Your Business

It happens at Disney because they encourage it in their culture and in their training, and because they set up systems to make sure it happens. Think about those systems.

What formal systems can you use to survey your customers?

How about creating an Advisory Council from some of your top customers to meet occasionally and provide input on your products and services?

Can you have your staff do an evaluation daily at the end of their shift, and note special problems? Will you make sure these are reviewed right then and that action is taken? That's what makes these work.

Disney Creates Magic Moments to Delight Guests

SWELTERING HOT temperatures occasionally hit Disneyland, and one such day led Lyn and Ron Dressler to buy ice cream treats from the street cart. Walking on, the sudden cold in her mouth caused Lyn pain, and made her dizzy and disoriented. Ron helped her sit on the steps at the side of the street to recover.

Moments later, a Disney security agent appeared, and advised that they couldn't sit there because it was a walkway.

Ron explained the situation and the cast member reacted immediately. He said to Lyn, "Press your tongue up against the roof of your mouth. It will help."

Lyn was amazed, as she was almost instantly relieved. "He was wonderful," she told me as she recalled the episode. "First he was doing his job, but as soon as he saw I was in distress, he came to my aid, and he knew what to do."

Ron chimed in, "I love Disneyland. My favorite time is at dusk when the lights on Main Street go on, but it's not quite dark. It's a magical time. But the real magic is how the employees are there to make our experience better. They are amazing."

In Disney language, it's called "Create a Magic Moment." Cast members are taught to make each guest contact a Magic Moment, because each interaction is an opportunity to add value to the visit.

"Happy birthday, Kysa!" My granddaughters were really surprised. Kysa and Rachel have close birthdays, and we had made that trip to Disneyland to celebrate. All afternoon, cast members had been wishing them happy birthday.

It started at lunchtime. As we were being seated for lunch, I told the server we were celebrating the birthdays. Moments later the server appeared with birthday stickers for each of them, and she had written their names on each sticker. She also brought them special desserts for the celebration.

The rest of the day, anytime a cast member spotted one of those birthday stickers, they said something special. The girls were thrilled.

It was another example of creating a Magic Moment. This time, the stickers made it easy, passing the "secret" to other cast members the rest of the day. The girls knew the secret, of course, and they loved it.

After we checked in at Disney's Grand Californian Hotel, as the bellhop escorted us to our room he gave us a gracious tour of the hotel, showing us various facilities and how to get from the hotel into the parks. We talked later about how wonderful it was, because it was more than just giving us the information. He seemed to really love the place and we felt he genuinely wanted us to have a good time.

The next afternoon, we were walking down the hallway toward our room, and one of the housekeeping staff looked at us, grinned, and asked, "Hi. Are you having fun today?"

I was astounded. Nowhere else has housekeeping staff cared or asked me if I was having fun.

They've all learned about the Disney culture, and they see their jobs as something more than providing assistance with luggage or cleaning services.

Disney tells their cast members, "Be aggressively friendly. Make each contact with a guest a Magic Moment." Note that being aggressively friendly doesn't mean "be aggressive." Disney encourages cast members to recognize a guest's state-of-mind, then react with appropriate friendliness. Someone in distress is looking for caring and help, not giggly enthusiasm. The appropriate response still requires making contact to determine how to assist.

At Disneyland there are lots of opportunities to meet Disney characters, and to get autographs or pictures. Often the actors who play these roles go beyond the duty of playing the role to playing with guests. It's a remarkable task, especially since most have to do it with no voice and no facial movement.

Once, over by the Enchanted Tiki Room, I saw Genie, from Aladdin, and Ballou, from The Jungle Book. A family of four was getting pictures.

First, they posed with Genie for a nice picture.

Then, they moved over to Ballou, and Genie helped them get in position. Just as they were ready to snap the picture, Genie stepped in front of them with his arms outstretched, blocking every face from the camera. His gracious behavior suddenly turned rude, but they all laughed, knowing it was a joke.

At that, Genie dropped to one knee, lowering himself and his arms so everyone was visible, beautifully posed with both Genie and Ballou.

The family laughed again, and the picture was snapped, probably one of the best photographs made that day. And the family will all remember the wonderful time they had with Ballou and the Genie.

Most Magic Moments are small interactions. Disney estimates that a guest in a theme park will have about 60 interactions with a cast member in a day. The goal is to make each of those interactions a Magic Moment.

Organizational Magic Moments

Disneyland has a parade called *Parade of the Stars*. It features a lot of Disney characters, but unlike older classic parades like the *Lion King Parade,* it doesn't really tell a spectacular story.

The Magic Moments in this parade come about because they recruit about 40 guests prior to the parade to participate. The guests put on special costumes and get a little dance instruction, and then the parade begins.

At four positions in the parade, the guest troupes appear, each doing their own musical "routine" with a cast member leader. Obviously amateurs, they have a wonderful time and it's a treat to watch them perform.

The last time I watched a line of guests bringing up the rear of the parade, carrying a line of rope that signified the end of the parade. They did a little dance routine as they marched.

One of the guests in that line was a young woman who was restricted to a wheelchair. As her wheelchair was pushed in the line to the music, she held and moved the rope in and out, up and down to the music along with the others, and was having the time of her life.

The company goes beyond expecting all the Magic Moments to be created by individual interactions with guests. The parade is an example of "organized" Magic Moments, experienced both by participating guests and those who watch the parade.

Disney strives to organize Magic Moments in three areas:

1. **High-Touch Magic Moments.** Participating in the parade would be a prime example of this. A high-touch Magic moment involves guest participation in an activity, beyond just being an observer or sitting on a ride.

2. **High-Show Magic Moments.** The parade itself could be considered a high-show Magic Moment, as could many of Disney's attractions and locations. These involve vivid presentations, colorful, lush, grand appearance and sound.

3. **High-Tech Magic Moments.** From making resort reservations, to checking in at the hotel and using the FastPass system, Disney has harnessed technology to build speed, accuracy, and expertise into service solutions.[19]

Clearly, many organizational Magic Moments are combinations of high-touch, high-show, and high-tech. For example, *Disney's Aladdin—A Musical Spectacular* at the Hyperion Theatre in the Hollywood Back-Lot at California Adventure park uses high tech to issue advance tickets and to count guests as they enter the audience queue. The production itself is a 40-minute high-show presentation equal to the elaborate Disney Broadway productions of *The Lion King* and *Beauty and the Beast.*

Some might say this is simply managing all the service functions of a business. But at Disney they want to make the experience *magical.* And they work hard to do exactly that.

Making Magic Moments is a major reason why cast members like their jobs; it's fun interacting with people, even though some guests may be less than friendly. It's also a major reason why guests love Disney attractions and list the friendly people as one of their favorite parts of the experience.

How You Can Create Magic Moments

Think of a Magic Moment as an interaction that creates value. That value may be fun, care, or relief.

As you look at the examples here, you can see that these are simple, everyday actions. Creating a Magic Moment doesn't have to be a big, involved event. It can be as simple as showing concern, or sharing in the fun.

You can create Magic Moments for your family, your friends, your coworkers, and your company's customers.

Be aggressively friendly. Look at interactions with others as an opportunity to create a Magic Moment.

Use Magic Moments in Your Company

Disney cast members try to create Magic Moments because it's part of the company culture. So the first step is defining the culture, and taking the steps to make it happen.

It's part of the training, and part of the daily banter among the cast.

Support systems also help. My granddaughters loved their birthday stickers, and the stickers had further value by taking the message to other cast members.

How do you suppose Disney trains housekeeping cast members to interact with guests in the way I experienced? It starts when they're first hired, and it continues.

You know their managers talk about it, and cast members must tell stories to one another about it.

It's all part of a management system that creates the right atmosphere for their cast members, in addition to planned systems. And the good news is that you can do it, too.

Four Keys to People Management

Oops! Standing in line for breakfast one Sunday morning at the River Belle Terrace Restaurant in Disneyland, I watched as pancakes were cooked.

Several cooks were on hand. One was a man, about 45 years old. Frankly, he was slow. And he wasn't making very good pancakes. Most of the pancakes he made were quickly thrown away by other cast members. It was a bit disconcerting.

The cast members acted normally, except they kept showing him how to pour a good pancake, and throwing out the ones he made.

Luckily, someone on the other side of the restaurant was cooking pancakes, too, or I might still be in that line. I couldn't help but wonder if that man ever reached the point that they could deliver his pancakes.

As I picked up my order, I asked the cast member about the man who was having so much trouble. I said, "Is he an executive from TDA getting a day in the park?"

"You guessed it," she laughed, and I remembered what I'd read about the requirement that the executives in the Team Disney Anaheim (TDA) administration offices get out for a day working the front lines every so often.

Get Out from Behind the Desk

When Disneyland was being built, Walt kept insisting that there should not be an administration building. "The public isn't coming here to see an administration building," he said. "Besides, I don't want you guys sitting behind desks. I want you out in the park, watching what people are doing and finding out how you can make the place more enjoyable for them."[20]

Today, Disney managers are expected to spend 70 per cent of their time in the operating areas of the park.

Think about some of the things that happen in the park.

Everyone helps clean the park. Everyone takes ownership of the cleanliness rule. And management sets the example; no one is exempt.

Eighty per cent of positions are filled from within.

Turnover is less than 20 per cent.

Seventy per cent of visitors return.

In the early days of the park, Walt realized that not everyone understood the dream, and that resulted in mistakes in guest service and attraction management. He asked C.V. Wood, Disneyland's first general manager, to resolve the problem. Van Arsdale France and Dick Nunis created programs that evolved into Disney University, the internal training organization that is still teaching classes called "Traditions," "Disney Way," and "You Create Happiness."

Four Elements of Disney People Management

Over time, the company has developed a powerful management system that capitalizes on the best of Walt's concepts, and compensates for his weaknesses. Positive reinforcement and communication are emphasized. It's a *system* that takes the culture and extends it to the entire park. The result is effective teamwork and an environment that cultivates loyalty. Their formula for successful management has four elements: Selection, Training, Communication, and Care.

Selection is about finding the right people for the company and the job. They call it "right-fit" selection. If the hiring process is organized correctly, the right people will be selected and they will fit into the organization well.

Training is about empowerment. Initial training will help someone new fit in, understand how they contribute to the company's goals, and give them required job skills.

Communication is about getting information to people and listening to what they have to say.

Care is about rewarding and providing positive reinforcement so people know when they're doing well and feel good about working for the company.

How to Use this at Home and at Work

How can you create a culture where you and those around you understand what's expected, and why?

How can you make it clear, in advance, what you expect from the people you interact with, and what they can expect from you?

How can you help people work on tasks that are right for them?

How can you focus on the things that matter to you and the people in your life?

What can you do to treat people with more respect?

How can you watch for signs of stress in yourself and in others, and what should you do about it?

How can you reward the people in your life on a daily basis?

How to Use this in Your Company

Here are some key points about applying the Disney system to your company:

1. Create a culture where the best people want to work for you.
2. Make it clear, in advance, what you expect from your new employees.
3. Pay attention to fitting people into the right job for them.
4. Indoctrinate new staff with your values early on.
5. Reinforce job training to focus on serving the customer.
6. Treat customer service staff with respect.
7. Train managers to watch for signs of stress.
8. Recognize good customer service in lots of ways.[21]

How 'Casting' Finds Champions to Run the Park

RECRUITING and selecting new employees in most companies is thought of as a "human resources" task.

At Disney theme parks, it's "casting." Most people who want to work at Disney are told to go the park's "Casting Center," a part of the recruiting department. At Casting, candidates will get a good look at how Disney employees behave. They will get a taste of Disney décor and enthusiasm. It's part of the show. As a result, training actually starts before an application is even filled out. Everything is carefully scripted.

At Disneyland and Walt Disney World the process differs a bit, but the essential process is like this:

First, consider who applies for a job with Disney. Because the company is so well known, nearly everyone has a pretty good idea of what the company does. They probably have a grasp of what the job would be like, at least to some degree. They've probably visited the park and feel they would fit in.

It's also very likely that they are coming in with a referral from another cast member. Disney has an aggressive referral program. At Disneyland, they tell their cast, "Our best new cast members come from your referrals. So don't miss out, be a Casting Scout!" Referrals are more likely to match the Disney culture, and are further enriched by having someone they already know on the inside who will help and encourage them in their new job.

At Walt Disney World, the first piece of paper a prospective employee gets at Casting starts with "Welcome... Casting is what we do. We're doing more than just filling hourly jobs, we're casting roles in our 'show' ... Because our show is very important to us, we are very careful and deliberate in the application process."

At the beginning of the hiring process, before filling out an application, they explain the "non-negotiables" of working with Disney. They use a video presentation to do this. It shows what it's like to work for Disney, and covers appearance, demeanor, service delivery, and benefits.

Ten per cent of applicants drop out right there. They might not like the rule about no beards. Or they might not like the work hours, or other aspects of the culture. At this point, there has been little cost to the company, so it's an advantage to let applicants sort themselves out right at the beginning.

The application has a section for "Personal Interests." Headings request information on hobbies, extracurricular activities, honors and awards, leadership positions, and languages. This helps the company determine which jobs, or roles, an applicant might fill.

In a one-on-one interview the interviewer focuses on work experience, personality, and education. Depending on the job and the applicant, a second interview might be required with managers from the area where the new cast member would be working. Some roles, especially dancers, vocalists, and musicians, require an audition before training.

New recruits are given a brochure about the "Disney Look." In this brochure, they explain that guests report the three things they like best about the Disney theme parks are the outstanding show, the cleanliness, and the friendly employees. They point out that the cleanliness is more than no litter on the streets, it's also the costumes and appearance of cast members.

The goal here is to select people who will enjoy working at Disney. These will be people who can "buy in" to the Disney culture and who should thrive on delivering the dream.

A synergy is realized when everyone hired is ready to be part of the culture. When they get together with other cast members, the enthusiasm spreads.

A newly hired cast member learned during the hiring process what is expected. And they quickly find that experienced cast members really do pick up trash, they really do try to make Magic Moments for guests, and they really do dress and groom themselves to fit the Disney image. It's easy for the new cast member to get a positive start.

"Right-fit" Casting

Behavior and preference tests are administered to match people to a job. For example, someone who will work backstage processing laundry needs to be the kind of person who can be committed to a repetitive task. Someone who is outgoing and finds it easy to talk to strangers would be matched to guest relations, marketing, or to a retail position.

Right-fit casting means matching people to jobs they will enjoy doing.

Nearly all management positions are filled from within. This provides managers more in tune with their staff, ready to spot fatigue or other problems and to step in to spell them when needed.

How to Use this at Home

Selection or casting is more important to your personal life than it might seem.

Disney employees affect each other. If one person is negative and refuses to meet the requirements, it affects others. It works like that in your home and with friends, too.

Can you think of a time when you've visited with friends who were complaining about their work, about their parents, about their spouses, or about politics? Can you recall joining in, either agreeing or coming up with examples of your own?

You see, it's normal for people to adapt themselves to "match" those around them. It's a sort of "Can you top this?" situation. Over a prolonged period, it can have a profound effect.

That's why parents caution their children to "hang out" with the right people, and avoid troublemakers and gang members. Children, and adults, become like the people they spend time with.

Who do you spend time with?

Are any of your friends or family negative, complaining, or rude to certain people? Do they fight, argue, or get angry often? If you spend time with people like that, you'll be like that, too. It will affect your behavior, your attitudes, and your values.

Spending time with negative people can lead to a downward spiral, leading to unhappiness and depression. On the other hand, being around positive people has the opposite effect and can help you emotionally onto an upward track.

Who *should* you spend time with?

You should spend your time with people who are like the person you want to be. You'll have to figure out who these people are for yourself.

Some things to consider: Successful. Happy. Productive. Friendly. People who dress well, because dress affects how you feel about yourself and how others think about you. People who make you and other people feel good. People who have good values.

It's easy to make excuses here, defending the wrong people just because they're friends, thinking that the friends are "okay" or that you're not affected. You'll often see this with your children, when you can clearly see the negative influence and they cannot. It's harder to see it in your own friends and even harder to take appropriate action.

What if important members of your family are the kind of people I'm telling you to avoid? Should you stay away from them?

That's a tough situation, and I'll tell you now, it's not easy. The answer is yes, you should avoid being around them too much, especially when they turn unpleasant.

I've got a couple of people like that in my family, and it *is* uncomfortable. Sharon and I visit them regularly, but as soon as they turn unpleasant, we look at our watches and gasp about the time, telling them we have to leave right away. And we leave immediately, no matter what's going on.

If they lived in the same house it would be harder, but we'd have to do the same thing. Even leaving quickly like we do, it has a negative effect on us and we have to work hard to overcome it.

How to Use this at Work

Let me share a story about a man who worked with me some years ago. At some point, he incurred the wrath of the receptionist whose desk was by the front door. She was always busy, and when he would come into the office she would complain and make demands on him that made him uncomfortable.

He overcame the problem by using the back door. He was able to minimize his exposure to a caustic personality and it helped him maintain a positive, productive attitude.

It's crucial at work to recognize this principle. To the extent possible, you must select the people you spend time with. Choose which people to ask for help, or to give assignments.

Going to lunch? Going to the water cooler, the smoking area, or the rest room? There's a saying, "Misery loves company." Watch who you end up spending your time with, because it will affect your attitude, your work, and how you feel.

How to Use this in Your Company

What are your processes and messages you send to potential employees? Do you consistently communicate your conditions of employment? Do you create a positive feeling?

What can you do to create a system for hiring that will weed out the *misfits* before you or they invest much time in the process? If yours is a small firm, you probably won't have a Central Casting office or a film to present what it's like to work at your firm, and to go over the requirements. Still, you can write up a document that goes over the company culture and requirements. Then you can ask an applicant to read through all that *before filling out an application.*

Anything you can do to discourage an applicant at the beginning will accomplish two things: First, it will let applicants "filter" themselves out of the process if they don't see themselves fitting into the company. Second, it establishes a behavior framework for the person if you do hire them; they will more readily adapt to the culture because they already know what is expected.

What about "right-fit," matching a new hire to a job that suits their personality and behavior?

Often a behavior profile or a values profile can reveal keys to motivation, job preference and compatibility. By matching an applicant's profiles to those of people already doing the job successfully, a "right-fit" selection is more likely. As a result, people like their jobs more and fit in more quickly.

Do you have formal, validated assessments that you use to see how well a person matches a job? Do you use this information to fit the right person into a compatible job, and further use it to assist in supporting and communicating with that person?

Disney's Secret Weapon: 'Traditions' Launches Careers

"INTRIGUING," I thought that morning as I stood in the Disney Gallery and read the story about Herb Ryman drawing the Disneyland schematic. Walt Disney called him in on a Saturday morning and spent the weekend describing what he envisioned for Disneyland. By Monday morning Ryman had completed an elaborate, detailed drawing, ready for presentation to potential investors.

Thirty minutes later I was in a charming restaurant in New Orleans Square with my friends Chip and Pat Rollins. As we ate, I overheard a server telling part of the story to the guests at a nearby table.

Chip was beginning to think of me as a Disney expert, and he asked me a question about the design of the park. I found myself telling the Ryman story. My guests were impressed, not realizing I had read the story less than an hour before. As I finished, I noticed the server who had been telling the story earlier was standing by our table, listening to my version.

As I finished, I turned to the server and asked, "How did I do, did I leave anything out?"

"You did great," he smiled, "I learned a few things myself!"

As I look back at that experience now, I recognize two things about that cast member:

First, by praising me he helped me enjoy a Magic Moment. I felt good, and Chip and Pat were further impressed.

Second, he knew the story.

It was a quick demonstration of two important principles of Disney magic. It raises the question, how does Disney manage to develop and maintain a huge organization where everyone is following the system so well?

"Training," is the easy answer, and certainly it's part of the culture that makes it work.

But a more precise answer would explain how the training is delivered, what's included, and how it works.

When a new cast member is hired, he or she has already been indoctrinated in the culture and in what it's like to work at Disney. The hiring process is carefully designed to set the stage for a quick but gentle transition into the Disney culture. The result? When the new hire shows up for their "first day," they expect to be trained, not quite realizing that the training was already underway.

Cast member training covers three areas, the past ("Traditions"), the present ("Operations"), and the future ("Vision").

Training the Culture

The first phase of training, an orientation program called "Traditions," connects new employees with the history, culture, and traditions of the company. It helps them see the "big picture" and how their role fits the company's activities.

All new hires go through this program, even top executives. There are no exceptions. Newly hired vice presidents sit next to mechanics and attraction hosts.

It's taught by frontline cast members, those who have the most guest contact. Disney found that professional trainers were not particularly successful with this program, due to an implied barrier between instructor and attendee.

The class includes films, discussions, company-based quizzes, property tours and a free lunch. It's a one-day program.

Each cast member is brought up to speed on the Walt Disney philosophy, mission, and values. They learn the history and even the trivia of the company. They discover that Disneyland is a stage and their job is putting on a show. The goal is creating happiness ("Magic Moments") more than serving food, parking cars, or counting money. It's the "Disney Way."

Cast members learn Disney's Service Theme and the four Service Standards.

Because it's a show, it must be rehearsed until it's right. Disney is immersed in "SOPs," standard operating procedures. The SOPs assure that there is a precise way to deliver at each attraction.

Traditions includes a look at the future of the company, so cast members can have a sense of what's coming and how they might fit in as the park continues to grow.

On-the-Job and Business Unit Training

After Traditions, cast members go to their work area to learn how to perform their specific role. Business Unit training consists of classes specific to skills needed in their new role. On-the-job training will last two days to two weeks, depending on the complexity of the new job. The best cast members are taken off the job to teach the new cast member the role and how it fits into the company culture.

By the end of this on-the-job training, the newest hires have the skills to handle nearly any situation at work and they have learned how those efforts contribute to the company's goals.

A card is provided as a reminder with a set of guidelines:

1. Make eye contact.
2. Greet and welcome each and every guest.
3. Seek out guest contact.
4. Provide immediate service recovery.
5. Display appropriate body language at all times.
6. Preserve the magical guest experience.
7. Thank each and every guest.[22]

Vision: Ongoing Training

Disney looks at the future and communicates it to cast members using a number of methods. They are concerned about where the company is going and what the future will mean to cast members.

In addition to periodic training, and training for new roles, they provide online, video, and CD classes for those who want to learn additional skills on their own time.

Trivia contests, celebrations, and other activities are designed to help cast members learn more about the company's history, traditions, and vision throughout their employment.

Career enhancement classes are offered. Disney "Foundations" is required for salaried staff, covering leadership and line of business.

Disney even makes it possible to earn a college degree through the resources of the company. They recognize that better educated cast members will enhance the capabilities of the organization.

So, it's no wonder that the cast member in that restaurant was ready to share the history of Disneyland, and promptly gave me a Magic Moment. His training for that skill started when he was first hired, and continued throughout his employment.

New Arrival Following

At Disneyland, new cast members are assigned to experienced staff in the recruiting department for six months. These people follow up on their training, their performance, and their adjustment. They are also available for questions.

Remember, Disney hires lots of young people to work in the park. For many it's their first job. They need to be taught something even more important that how the culture works, and how to do the job. They need to be taught how to go to work. Many haven't yet learned that they're counted on every day they're scheduled, and that they're needed on time. So, there's an effort made to teach and follow up on those skills.

How to Use this at Home

Training yourself for your personal life? Is there a personal application here? Sure!

Give some thought to your personal and family history, to your philosophy, to your dreams and goals. Think about your future, and how you want your life to work.

Start a notebook and in that notebook create sections for History, Traditions, Actions, and Vision. Make notes in those sections about what you know already, and try to develop more.

As you think about it, continue to make notes of it in your notebook. You'll end up with a book that tells more about you than most people ever know about themselves.

You'll discover where you're on target, and where you're missing the mark. You'll be able to take action and make decisions, small or large, that further your personal dreams and goals.

Now think about how you're going to share that with the people close to you.

Your family deserves to know what you're thinking, and where you're going. If they can share your dreams, they can provide emotional support and assistance.

And you'll have more fun and find more satisfaction.

Think, too, about what training you're going to need to accomplish what you want. Is it a college degree, or a trade school? Maybe it's something you can learn for free studying at the public library. Or maybe it's something you can learn from other people.

When your dream and vision are clear, you'll be amazed how other people will appear to help.

How to Use this at Work

Unless you work at Disney or a company with a similar process, you probably know very little about the company's history, traditions, and culture. Your training has probably missed this information, or given it brief attention.

I hope I have impressed on you how important it is. So here's what I'd like to suggest.

Start a notebook and in that notebook create sections for History, Traditions, Actions, and Vision. Make notes in those sections about what you know already, and try to discover more.

As you learn more, continue to make notes of it in your notebook.

In the process, you'll learn more about the company, and come to know it better than nearly anyone else.

You'll discover where it's on target, and where it's missing the mark. You'll be able to take action and make suggestions and decisions, small or large, consistent with your position, that further the company's dreams and goals.

At some point, if you're asked to help a new employee adjust to their new job, you'll be in a unique position to sit down with them and visit about the company and give them a big head start toward fitting in and becoming an asset.

They'll also have more fun and find more job satisfaction, and you will too.

How to Use this in Your Company

At most companies, new hire training is task oriented, designed to show a person "how" to do a job, more than "why." The typical first day on the job is all about filling out paperwork, getting security id cards, and finding the proper workplace.

Some more enlightened companies do quick "how-to" training, then assign a "buddy" to the new employee. Often the buddy is busy elsewhere.

Very few companies put any real emphasis on the company's history, traditions, and culture. It may take new hires years to figure out how it all works. If they stay that long, what they learn probably won't be what the company intends.

Have you written out the history of your company, including the dreams, the vision, and the philosophy?

Have you defined what's expected?

Is this a key part of both your first day training and your continuing training?

Do you insist that everyone in the firm participates, and continues to participate?

How are your training methods packaged and presented? What's the content? How is it timed?

Everything speaks of your true company culture, so make certain it's what you want it to be.

Eyes & Ears and Bulletin Boards

OMINOUS SMOKE was beginning to seep from around a food warmer at La Petite Patisserie in New Orleans Square. As the smoke increased, the manager called the Disneyland emergency phone number and ordered an evacuation of the area.

Moments later, supervisors from around the park were running in all the doors. The message had gone out instantly, and the response was immediate. A minute or two later, the Disney fire crews arrived.

It was a minor wiring problem, and the main result was a lot of smoke.

The key observation was the fast communication. Supervisors from around the park reacted in seconds, even ahead of the fire crews.

Every company and every organization – even a family – thrives or suffers based on the quality of their communication.

The smoke in New Orleans Square demonstrates that Disney's emergency communication is effective. For emergencies, they have an emergency phone line, and dispatching is done via pager. Codes are used to quickly identify the severity, location, and nature of the problem.

Share the Valuable Information

The people in a company thrive on information, and starve when information is withheld. Yet many firms tend to keep information hidden from employees, letting the rumor mill spread the word inaccurately. Disney works to overcome that with a variety of day-to-day communication methods designed to match the needs of the cast.

A simple cork bulletin board is one of the most effective ways communication travels throughout the company. Boards are installed in various cast work areas where cast members can read pertinent information for their area.

For example, after parades the director's notes are pinned to a bulletin board for review by participating cast members. Both positive and negative comments are posted. Cast members gather around the board to see how things went and to learn what needs to happen for the next parade.

At Disneyland a newsletter, the *Disneyland Line,* is distributed weekly. At Walt Disney World it's a similar publication, *Eyes & Ears.* This makes it easy to keep cast informed about progress regarding issues raised in the annual survey, traditions, day-to-day operation, and plans for the future. They add profiles of cast members, classified ads, and job listings.

Kiosks are provided that are stocked with insurance forms, change in benefits forms, tax forms, etc. As a result, cast members have a "self-service" Human Resources department, at least for forms and brochures.

In California, a pocket-sized *Cast Member Reference Guide* is produced weekly, packed with schedules and specific information of use to cast members and for cast members to tell guests. In Florida they call it *Tell-A-Cast,* and produce a different guide for each theme park.

These all get information from managers to cast members.

Everyone has valuable information to share. Disney thrives on the input of their cast members, because the cast knows better than anybody else what's going on in the company. The cast also needs to know their efforts contribute to the organization's success.

Recognizing this, Disney has developed a number of methods that enable two-way communication.

Communication Up the Line

There's an annual survey, the "Cast Excellence Survey." Disney contracts this with an outside company. It's voluntary; 80 per cent of cast members respond. After results are tabulated, the results are shared with the cast. Groups of cast members then help to develop action plans.

One question repeated every year on the cast survey is "How do you want to hear information about the company?" For decades the top answer has always been, "From my leader." Disney insists that managers spend 70 per cent of their time in the operating area.

Suggestion boxes are used to uncover emerging issues and address them early on.

In the Disney Stores they use a Cast Member Communication Log, a binder used to communicate information between the management team and fellow cast members. It's read, noted, and initialed by every cast member at the beginning and end of every shift. In this binder managers can note unusual concerns for cast members starting a shift. At the end of a shift, cast members can rate their shift on various 1-10 scales and note any particular problems that need to be addressed.[23]

Disney uses "What's on your mind?" forms to gather concerns and ideas from cast members.

Coaching

Cast members who work backstage need to understand how important their work is to the company. Being isolated from guest areas makes this hard, so when managers go "onstage," they take backstage workers with them to see how the work is received. It helps them see the "big picture."

Laundry workers will be shown the areas where the laundry is stored and where it is used. Kitchen staff will be shown the banquet room before or during an event.

How to Use this at Home

Communication at home is critical. Lots of couples and families use a bulletin board to post notes to each other, work schedules, and a calendar with scheduled appointments, parties, and events.

How to Use this in Your Company

Think about the systems you could put in place to improve communication. Lots of companies think that voice mail, email, pagers, or cell phones solve everything, but they may not be ideal.

Consider Disney's methods listed here. Would a bulletin board help? What about a company newsletter? Have you considered a communication log in a binder? What about a suggestion system? Or a kiosk that supplies employee forms and information?

The Amazing System that Takes Care of the Cast

IN THE STUDIO and at Disneyland, hundreds of artists, technicians, and managers functioned together to deliver the dream. Walt would push and criticize. He seldom praised one's work directly, though he might tell someone else. Many flourished, but not all.

At one point, Walt confessed, "I've been a slave driver.[24]" He could crowd others out of a project and create resentment. It was important to agree with his ideas, yet he admonished any of his staff who he thought was becoming a "yes man."

In spite of having an amazing ability to inspire his staff, Walt could be manipulative, praising a guy one day and ignoring him the next. And he was prone to put someone down in public, even management.

This, perhaps, was Walt's greatest flaw.

The company has responded by providing multiple systems to praise and reward cast members for their good efforts, big and small. And it's made Disney a remarkable place to work.

Former cast members tend to talk about the experience like this:

"I know that there will never be anything like that in my life again. I thank god every day for giving me the opportunity."

"We have, probably, the most impact on somebody's life that one can have."

"I will never forget the magical role that I played in two little children's lives. They will probably come back there in the future

with their families and remember that one person helped them out when they needed it."

At Disney, "Care" means recognize, reward, and celebrate for customer satisfaction, performance, behavior, and employment tenure.

Recognition

Distinguished service awards start with a special pin at one year, then at five years and every five years after that. After ten years, an annual banquet is given.

Perfect attendance awards, cast member of the month, and peer recognition systems abound.

Three Times as Much Positive Feedback

The goal at Disney is to hand out lots of positive rewards and recognition. Can this mean there's never any negative feedback? No. Disney managers have to provide corrective instruction when it's needed, but there's a goal: Provide at least three times as much positive feedback as negative.

In most jobs, employees hear about it when things are going wrong, and they hear nothing when they're doing their jobs well. That absence of feedback is supposed to be a good thing, but it's not. Positive feedback will do wonderful things. Disney has lots of systems to accomplish this.

Lets look at a few of the systems.

Guest Service Fanatic Cards

At Walt Disney World, managers and lead hosts carry little cards which they use any time they catch a cast member doing something especially well.

Managers fill the card out, including the specific thing that earned the recognition, and give it to the cast member.

Cast members can keep the card or put it in a special entry box in their work area. Each month there's a big celebration, and a drawing, and 5 or 6 names are drawn from all the cards that were put in boxes. There's music, and Mickey or a top exec draws the winning card. The winners get prizes, like a new TV or a Disney gift set. Those with more cards get more opportunities to win. So... they're recognized, rewarded, and they celebrate.

This is a powerful method of recognition and reward, and it meets several criteria that are important for effective positive feedback: It's positive, it's immediate, and it's specific.

Congratulations!
You have been recognized as a Guest Service Fanatic for:

_____

*Name:*_____

*Department:*_____

*Recognized by:*_____ *Date:*_____

Managers are expected to hand out cards many times each day. A quota of 10 cards a day per manager suggests that Disney expects and finds a considerable amount of extraordinary performance.

In some areas, special pins are awarded to cast members who have accumulated 25, 50, or 75 Guest Service Fanatic cards. The pins are extremely rare and are only handed out to the "Cream of the Crop," or those Cast Members that have consistently gone above and beyond in the area of Guest/Cast service.

The Guest Service Fanatic card program has an additional benefit: It focuses managers on catching people doing something right. For a manager who otherwise tends to become focused on problems, this can be a very empowering adjustment.

Applause-O-Gram

At Walt Disney World, when a cast member goes above and beyond the expected performance and does outstanding work, the Applause-O-Gram is written up for on the spot recognition.

It's posted on the work area bulletin board and a copy goes in the personnel file.

Spirit of Disney Award

The Spirit of Disney award is given to exceptional Disneyland cast members who qualify to win the highest award bestowed upon a cast member by the Walt Disney Company. Cast members must be nominated for award by another cast member; then a management committee decides on actual recipients. Fewer than one per cent of cast members win, and it can be won only once in a lifetime.

At a special awards banquet, the winner is presented with a special pin, and guests of the winning cast member receive a different pin to commemorate the event.

Disney Ambassador

The Ambassador Program is the pinnacle of achievement for any Disney cast member. They compete to fulfill the duties of this coveted role, acting as Ambassador for their particular resort. Duties include making public appearances, escorting V.I.P.'s, attending important park functions and local community events, and travelling to various locales to promote Disney and it's wholesome family brand of entertainment.

A special pin is worn on the Ambassador's lanyard and is provided to cast members who have a special relationship with the Ambassador Program.

The first Disneyland Ambassador was Julie Reihm in 1965. There is only one Ambassador per resort, which means one each for Walt Disney World, Disneyland, Tokyo Disneyland, and Disneyland Paris. Each selected Cast Member serves in that capacity for one year.

Partners in Excellence

Disney created a special award for cast members called Partners in Excellence. Candidates are nominated by other cast members, and evaluated by a committee of other cast members. Key behaviors, which are the foundation for the three pillars of Performance Excellence, include:

- Cast Excellence
- Guest Satisfaction
- Operational Excellence

Winners are given a special pin, a statue, and banquet celebration. Second time winners get a second-level pin, banquet, and a two-night resort vacation for two.

Letters from guests

When guests send letters to Disney and single out cast members for having provided an exceptional experience, the company makes a big deal out of it. Letters are posted on bulletin boards and cast members get recognition.

It's Fun

Work is made fun, and that spills over into giving customers a fun experience.

Even backstage the cast members have fun. Gardeners make fun of their topiary and parking lot workers keep score on how many people they spot doing "non-Disney" activities in their cars on the parking lot.

They have lots of staff parties and special events like canoe races. One former cast member says it can be too much fun at times. "It's like being in college, with all the parties," she says.

Disney's published standards say guests will receive the right quality of treatment when cast members are treated to the same standards.

The result is a caring organization.

How to Use this at Home and at Work

Think about what you might be able to do to recognize the good things that people in your life do, whether they're doing it for you, for themselves, or for someone else.

If a Disney manager can do it, you can do it, too.

Set a goal to find ten people every day doing something good, and praise them for it. Keep a list each day, so you can look at it in the evening and check your count.

Think about it. Can you tell a spouse they did something well? Can you thank the mail carrier for handling a special package? Can you thank your child, or a friend, for doing something well?

At work you could thank your boss, your coworkers, delivery people, and vendors. Thank a customer for something they do that's different and special.

At school thank a teacher, or a fellow student. Thank the support staff. Praise someone for being excellent.

Learn to watch for people doing something outstanding, and praise them for it. Ten times a day. Keep a list and review it at the end of the day.

It will make them feel good, and you'll feel good, too.

How to Use this in Your Company

"Catching someone doing something outstanding" can make a major difference in your business.

What can you do to create a system so you and your managers are looking for people who do good things? Disney's Guest Service Fanatic program is powerful.

Maybe you could have business cards printed that say, "Wow! You have been recognized for…" and fill them out to give to staff who are doing good things. You could even give cards to vendors, customers, and outside support people.

We developed *Major Magic Moment*™ cards for our clients. They're amazingly effective.

A Major Magic Moment card program will have your staff focusing on customers and ways to give them outstanding service. And it will have you and your managers focusing on catching staff doing outstanding things, instead of catching them doing something wrong.

This will positively affect both staff and managers, and improve morale overall.

Finally, like Disney, you can have a monthly drawing from the Major Magic Moment cards and give a free dinner for two, a gift certificate, or other special award at a monthly staff celebration.

The monthly celebration is important. Have refreshments and make it a party. That reinforces the message that it's important to excel.

What other awards can you create to recognize and celebrate the outstanding things your people do?

Look at the many Disney programs. Each is positive, but not spectacular. What's spectacular is that they actually do use all these ideas.

What ideas can you adapt for use in your company?

Take the Risk and Pay the Bills

WITH ONLY $40 in his pocket, Walt Disney left for California in 1923. Arriving, he visited his older brother, Roy, in the hospital. He told Roy he needed help; Roy checked out of the hospital and joined Walt as a partner in his animation enterprise, investing $200.

Originally the studio was called the Disney Bros. Studio. Walt became the artist and producer, and Roy handled finance. Roy became the financial wizard behind the Disney success. He secured desperately needed loans to fund Walt's cutting edge animation projects and to build needed studios. At a time when he still opposed the project, he nailed down the deal with ABC for the Disneyland partnership.

Roy was against Disneyland from the start; it was such a departure from the film business. Even after he negotiated the deal that funded initial construction, he had doubts. Finally, on opening day, when he encountered freeways and highways jammed with people trying to get to Disneyland, he was relieved and jubilant, recognizing that it might work after all.

After Walt's death in 1966, when it came time to build the Florida project, Roy created a remarkable financial plan to fund it and later named it "Walt Disney World" out of respect for his brother.

A Balance Between Dreaming and Practicality

To Walt's dreamer, Roy was the antagonist, always practical, wanting to avoid the risk. The pattern was repeated for nearly every new project. Walt would dream it. Roy would question the costs and oppose it. This would spur Walt on to develop the concept and make it worthy. Finally, Roy would relent and find the money to make it happen.

This rivalry between siblings created an interesting balance. Because of Roy's opposition, Walt was forced to examine his ideas carefully. Walt was persistent and would push Roy to win approval. In the process, Walt had to make sure the public would respond and that the project would benefit the company and its customers. There were probably projects that were dropped because he was unable to justify them to his brother, but we don't find those in biographical accounts.

Because of Walt's urging, Roy was constantly challenged to find ways to fund new projects. Without the urging of a younger brother who he loved and respected, Roy might have been able to hold the company back by limiting the activities and stopping the very projects that made the company grow and, ultimately, made it financially secure.

At times the feud was bitter. There were times the brothers would avoid each other and barely speak; one such episode lasted several years.

Through all the disagreements, the brothers stayed together, and Walt Disney Productions thrived. In all likelihood, neither brother could have created the dynamic Disney organization without the other.

Walt once said of Roy, "If it hadn't been for my big brother, I swear, I'd have been in jail several times for check bouncing."

And Roy liked to say of his loyalty to Walt, "My brother made me a millionaire. Why shouldn't I be?"[25]

How to Use this at Home

I'm sure it was emotionally draining to Walt and Roy to be at odds as much as they were. If your household has one partner who's a dreamer and wants to spend it all, and another partner who wants to be more practical, investing and accumulating capital, you know just how they felt. It might be valuable for both partners to read this book, then discuss the situation.

If your household has two partners who agree to spend it all, or to save it all, there's less conflict, but there may still be frustration, either for being broke, or for leading a dull life.

If you are the household, and you don't have to get a partner to agree, then all the responsibility rests with you.

The key to success here is more than a compromise between the two positions. Think about the process between Walt and Roy:

1. Dream.
2. Question costs and oppose until it makes sense.
3. Persistent development of the plan until it's practical.
4. Find the money to make it work.

It makes sense to approach your personal "business" just as Walt and Roy did. You may not accomplish every dream; I'm sure Walt gave up on lots of ideas that wouldn't prove themselves worthy of Roy's tests. But a lot of good things can happen when you're willing to dream wonderful things and pursue the right dreams in an effective manner.

How to Use this in Your Company

It's a certain formula for bankruptcy when you let the dreamers spend all the money any way they want to. The money and the credit line will be gone in no time, and there will be little to show for it.

It's equally destructive to let the accounting people run the show. If every move has to be a proven step with a low-risk return, the rate of return will be low, probably lower than the inflation rate. So the company will still fail.

In recent years, especially in public companies, management has been increasingly pressured to show immediate profits. The management style that thrives in that atmosphere is likely to cut back on development and quality initiatives, and to block any radical new projects. The high-tech dot-com failures of 2000-2001 strengthened that conservative approach; it was one area where risks were taken, and results not realized.

The key is balance and process. In your company you want to be sure there is a good balance of risking and protecting, and that you go through a process to select projects and increase the likelihood of success. The Disney formula is a good one and can be used by anyone:

1. Dream and propose a project.
2. Question costs and oppose until profits are likely.
3. Persistent development of the plan until it's practical.
4. Find the money to make it work.

Even with Success in Your Blood, You Can Fail

I LOVE Disneyland, both for entertainment and as a business model. As I've continued to gush about Disney, you might have gotten the idea that I'm not aware that some things are not perfect in pixie land.

Please understand, I'm in love with Disneyland, both for entertainment and as a business model. But I know there have been mistakes. I also know any organization of people, whatever the size, will have its bad moments.

Yes, I'm aware that in spite of Disney's amazing approach to people management, some people are unhappy, for all the variety of problems that people become disenchanted with their jobs anywhere. I've hired and fired people, and met a payroll, so I know how tough it can be.

It's interesting that many of the people who have spoken badly of Disney still say they value the fact that they worked there. Or they might indicate they would go back. It seems to get in their blood, creating a loyalty unique to Disney.

So there are glitches. I understand that.

They also make mistakes, and the further they've strayed from the Walt Disney formula, the tougher it's been.

Rocket Rods

A prime example is Rocket Rods. The attraction opened May 22, 1998, the centerpiece of a big overhaul of Tomorrowland.

It seemed like a good idea.

Unfortunately, Disney didn't provide much of a budget, so the new "high speed" rocket cars were engineered to run on the old slow-speed PeopleMover track. The track had no banked curves, so the rods had to slow down to take turns, then speed up again. Tracks were difficult to maintain. This served to make the ride less fun and more prone to breakdown. The ride was closed most of the time, and was finally abandoned in September, 2000.

Disneyland President Cynthia Harriss said, "The high-speed attraction was never able to perform to its designed show standards." The problem, she said, was a budget-conscious decision to run the high-speed Rods on the unbanked track.[26]

California Adventure

A more serious problem was the concept at California Adventure, the new park opened next door to Disneyland in 2001. Disney boasts of investing $1.4 billion in the new park, but that includes construction of the Grand Californian Hotel and a Downtown Disney district with retail stores and restaurants. Those two parts of the project have been received well, but the new park has enjoyed lackluster attendance.

Frankly, I like the new park, but when I visit Anaheim I spend most of my time at Disneyland.

Some have questioned the concept, a park in California about California. Epcot's international district in Florida is hugely successful because it brings an authentic sample of other countries to the guests, creating a unique experience. Perhaps a California Adventure park should have been built in Europe, and a European Adventure park built in California.

More certain is this: the attractions were developed on a budget. One of the executives was quoted in the planning days saying, "Make it as good as Magic Mountain." That they probably did, but they put it next door to Disneyland, the first and most well known theme park in the world.

There are fewer rides than next door at Disneyland, and for the most part, they forgot to tell a story. California Adventure has Grizzly River run, a wet and wild water ride with hardly a story; Disneyland has Splash Mountain, a great water ride with an elaborate story inside the mountain.

Throughout Disneyland that amazing 90-80-60% perspective building technique was used to create an unreal, storybook feeling. California Adventure seems to not have that feature.

California Adventure has one big roller coaster, plus one Wild Mouse type coaster, much like you'd find at any amusement park in California or across the US. Disneyland has Thunder Mountain Railroad, Matterhorn, Space Mountain, and Indiana Jones.

Guests at the entrance walk up to a ticket booth and are given a choice: Buy a ticket to Disneyland, with more cool "E-ticket" rides, rides that tell better stories, rides you've experienced before; or, choose California Adventure, with a few rides, some audience sit-down shows, and rides that don't tell as good a story.

"Oh, the price is the same, which ticket do you want?"

Cynthia Harriss insists, "We've got a good product." That's true, but Disneyland, next door at the same price, has a *great* product.

Given time, Disney will figure out how to make the concept work. Attractions are already being hastily added and enhanced. Occasionally, on busy days at Disneyland, they open the California Adventure park to Disneyland visitors without an additional charge. The "California Adventure" theme will probably be modified, while retaining the name.

In earlier days, Walt would insist it be done right, whatever the cost, and Roy would insist that it makes business sense, then find the money somewhere.

Not the Perfect Place to Work

Occasionally there's talk about how bad it is to work at Disneyland or Walt Disney World, that the hours are "crazy," the pay is low, and the benefits are inadequate. Like most companies, entry-level cast members get the worst schedules. One 20-year Disney veteran told me, "We have to prepare them for Mom to be unhappy when the holidays come around, because they will be working the holidays as well as the weekends."

When you examine with other amusement parks, theatres, foodservice companies, resort hotels, and retail stores, wages and schedules compare favorably. Benefits match or exceed the others. And for some, the Disney experience makes it all worthwhile. Others take the lessons learned to other jobs and say the "Disney education" was invaluable.

The proof of Disney's success lies in the tenure of their employees. On a recent trip to Disneyland I met a cast member at the Blue Bayou Restaurant who had been with there seven years.

My server had been there six years. When I had breakfast at the Carnation Café my server said he started working at Disneyland for a summer job and had been there 28 years. When he saw that impressed me, he introduced me to another server working that morning who had been there a year longer, and told me the chef, Oscar, had been there 47 years.

Later in the day I asked three more cast members how long they had been there. Their answers were two years, 20 years, and two months. This is not a sign of a company with a turnover problem.

Ask that question next time you're at a movie theatre, resort hotel, or restaurant. High turnover is the norm in the industry. I asked a cast member from Disney recruiting if they had a problem with turnover, and she answered, "Well, yes, turnover is a problem." But her perspective is recruiting, and she's never worked anywhere but Disney.

Over at Disney Imagineering where they design and build the attractions, they work in a slightly different world. It's a creative environment, and creative minds thrive.

However, when Disney cuts the investment in development, the Imagineering staff gets cut.

"My husband was a Disney Imagineering employee for 10 years, designing special effects for the rides, and he just got laid off with no warning," one woman told me. "He worked 12 to 14 hours a day on installation of shows and then they just kicked him out." It's part of an intensive downsizing at Imagineering, she said. "There used to be 2000 People at Imagineering; it is now down to 800!"

Of course, downsizing during certain economic downturns is common in American business. And with Disney's movie business heritage, they tend to look at attraction development like producing a movie. With movies, studios generally hire the staff they need for the project, and they're let go when it's done. That may also be part of the reasons movies have become so expensive to produce.

Is Imagineering work like producing a movie (a project), or is it more like doing ongoing research? It's probably some of both.

It brings up the classic business school debate: How much can you cut research to save short term money without hurting the company in the long term? On one hand, they finished building a theme park (California Adventure) so they may not need as much effort in Imagineering. On the other hand, that park still needs development work to make it successful and there's always Walt's admonition, "Disneyland [and the other Disney parks] will never be finished."

The Eisner Era

I've heard many stories about Walt wandering through Disneyland, talking to attraction hosts and guests. Walt would even spend the night in a little apartment upstairs over the fire department in the Main Street U.S.A. area. It kept him in touch with the business.

Michael Eisner came from Paramount to Disney as CEO in 1984. At that point, the company was ailing, mostly because of a declining movie business. From 1985 to the early 1990s, the company prospered, primarily from successful movie production. Also during that time high tech attractions were added to the Disney theme parks.

In recent years, Eisner has come under attack. Critics question his high pay (about six million dollars in 2002) when the company was doing well. As earnings fumbled and the stock price declined, pressure increased. The resulting changes include park development controlled by budgetary considerations and the R&D cuts at Imagineering.

In biographical reviews about Eisner, there's little mention of theme parks. Yet the theme parks division is usually the company's most profitable, and provides a steady income less dependent on the success of the more volatile movie business or on varying advertising revenues. As Walt Disney discovered in the few years after Disneyland opened in 1955, the theme park business gave the company financial stability that did not exist in movie production.

I know Eisner makes it to Disneyland on occasion; I wonder how often he wanders through Disneyland like Walt did, alone and unannounced, to stay in touch with the business.

No More Excuses

REINVENTING how you do things may be troubling. So often, a decision is made, but the decision is halfhearted or it's not executed well and by the next week it's business as usual.

You can bring magic into your life at home, and at work. If you run a company, you can apply the Disney magic there.

It's something Walt Disney did well. He did it in cartoon animation, feature films, television, and theme parks. More than once he risked his entire company on an innovative dream.

Disney's Success Formula has three components:

1. Quality Guest Experience
2. Quality Cast Experience
3. Quality Business Practices

In this book we've looked at all three, with emphasis on the first two. We examined what they do, and how they do it.

Much of what's been presented here seems like common sense. But it's not really very common. The difference is simple: At Disney, they actually do it!

I'm eager for you to take what's presented here and use it to make your life and your business better!

Bringing about change in an organization can be a daunting task. It's critical to have employee participation. Consider these points:

1. Changing a corporate culture takes time.
2. There must be real benefits to everyone involved.

3. Management must consistently model the desired behavior.

4. There must be top management commitment at the outset.[27]

Since this book is intentionally thin, so that it's quick to read and easy to carry with you, it's necessary to provide you with additional resources to assist in your endeavors. I'm excited to be able to do that in a dynamic and adaptive way.

I want to stay in touch with you and help you achieve all your dreams, your goals, your desires. I also want you to share with me your success stories and let you read the stories of others. For this purpose we have created a special website:

www.MagicStrategy.com

There you'll find a free exercise designed to enhance your ability to apply the ideas found in this book. To access the special section for readers who have finished the book click on the "Members" button. Your special access code is 1955. If you've paid attention, you'll remember the significance of that number, and that's why we used it as an access code.

This book is intentionally short; at the website you'll find additional information about using these methods.

Apply these ideas in your life.

This information will help you in countless ways, so keep your copy of this book close and refer to it often.

Share this information with others in your family, your company, your school, or your organization. As more people adopt these methods, the resulting synergy will create remarkable results.

Suggested Reading

Books and Audio

Adventures in Creative Thinking, audio by Mike Vance

Be Our Guest, book by the Disney Institute

The Disney Version, book by Richard Schickel

The Disney Way, book by Bill Capodagli and Lynn Jackson

Inside the Dream: The Personal Story of Walt Disney, book by Katherine Barrett, Richard Greene, and Katherine Greene

Inside the Magic Kingdom: Seven Keys to Disney's Success, book by Tom Connellan

The Magic Kingdom: Walt Disney and the American Way of Life, book by Steven Watts

The Man Behind the Magic: The Story of Walt Disney, book by Katherine Greene and Richard Greene

Mouse Tales: A Behind the Ears Look at Disneyland, book by David Koenig

Prince Of The Magic Kingdom: Michael Eisner And The Re-Making Of Disney, book by Joe Flower

Remembering Walt: Favorite Memories of Walt Disney, book by Amy Boothe Green and Howard E. Green

Walt Disney: An American Original, book by Bob Thomas

Walt Disney: Famous Quotes

Walt Disney Imagineering: A Behind the Dreams Look at Making the Magic Real, book by The Imagineers and C. E. Jones

Internet Resources

Disney Online: http://www.disney.com

Disneyland Inside & Out: http://www.intercotwest.com

Mouse Planet: http://www.mouseplanet.com

Mike Vance: http://www.creativethinkingassoc.com

Special website for readers of this book:

      http://www.MagicStrategy.com

Notes

1 *The Magic Kingdom,* by Steven Watts (Houghton Mifflin, 1997), p.384.
2 *The Magic Kingdom,* by Steven Watts (Houghton Mifflin, 1997), p.397.
3 *The Magic Kingdom,* by Steven Watts (Houghton Mifflin, 1997), p.403.
4 Exhibit at Disney Gallery, Disneyland, 2001.
5 Disneyland Cast Referral card, 2003.
6 *Adventures in Creative Thinking,* audio by Mike Vance, 1977.
7 *Walt Disney,* by Robert Thomas (Hyperion, 1997), p. 263.
8 *Walt Disney Imagineering,* by the Imagineers (Disney Editions, 1996), p. 9.
9 *Walt Disney: Famous Quotes* (Disney Kingdom Editions, 1999), p. 166.
10 *Be Our Guest,* Disney Institute (Disney Press, 2000), p. 57.
11 *Inside the Dream: The Personal Story of Walt Disney,* by Katherine and Richard Greene (Disney Editions, 2001), p. 60.
12 *Be Our Guest,* Disney Institute (Disney Press, 2000), p. 29-35.
13 *The Disney Version,* by Richard Schickel (Ivan R. Dee, 1997), p. 147-148.
14 *The Magic Kingdom,* by Steven Watts (Houghton Mifflin, 1997), p.372.
15 *The Magic Kingdom,* by Steven Watts (Houghton Mifflin, 1997), p.405.
16 *Walt Disney,* by Robert Thomas (Hyperion, 1997), p. 244.
17 *Walt Disney,* by Robert Thomas (Hyperion, 1997), p. 325.
18 Bruce Jones, Disney Institute, presentation to HSM Cultura & Desenvolvimento, 2001
19 *Be Our Guest,* Disney Institute (Disney Press, 2000), p. 188.
20 *Walt Disney,* by Robert Thomas (Hyperion, 1997), p. 263.
21 "Casting for Customer Service," by Tony Mosely, The Service Excellence Experience
22 "Casting for Customer Service," by Tony Mosely, The Service Excellence Experience
23 Traditions/Magic Handbook, The Disney Store (1997), p. 18, 55.
24 *The Magic Kingdom,* by Steven Watts (Houghton Mifflin, 1997), p.192.
25 *The Magic Kingdom,* by Steven Watts (Houghton Mifflin, 1997), p.430-431.
26 Disney press release, May 3, 2001.
27 *The Disney Way,* by Bill Capodagli & Lynn Jackson (McGraw-Hill, 1999), p. 28-29.

"Walt always asked you to do something that was far beyond what you thought you were capable of doing, and he always made you surprise yourself by reaching that goal." — Alice Davis

About the Author

Rich Hamilton brings you over 30 years experience as a speaker, entrepreneur, and expert in sales, marketing, and advertising. Rich has authored over 500 articles and produced and appeared in over 3000 radio programs. He was president of a broadcast communications company, is a qualified systems analyst, and has consulted with hundreds of companies seeking to help them increase their sales and profits through advertising, marketing, and selling.

Rich Hamilton is available for a limited number of speaking engagements each year.

Richard Hamilton Associates offers behavior and values profiles for staff selection and management; learning systems for sales, marketing, and advertising; and consulting services.

Contact Information:

Richard Hamilton Associates
Phone: 602.438.2345 1.800.816.7710
Internet: www.SellBetter.com
Email: info@MagicStrategy.com
Mail Care of: SellBetter, Box 50186, Phoenix, AZ 85076

The Magic Moment Recognition Package

We've put together a special package for managers who want to implement a recognition program combining elements similar to Walt Disney World's Guest Service Fanatic card program and the Applause-O-Gram program. The Magic Moment Starter Pack Includes:

- 5,000 full-color pocket-size Major Magic Moment cards.
- 150 full-color Applause-O-Gram Recognition Certificates.
- 6 copies of *Disney Magic-Business Strategy* book.
- 1 copy of *Disney Magic-Business Strategy* audio cassette program.
- The Special *Magic Moment Recognition Program Manual* to use in implementation of the program, including checklists, a special audio cassette program describing how the programs work and how to coordinate them in various sizes of companies, and information about special recognition pins and periodic celebration meetings.

How to Get Other Products

Order additional copies of this book or our other products from the web site, by mail or by phone:

www.MagicStrategy.com

SellBetter Tools, Box 50186, Phoenix, AZ 85076

Tel. 800.434.1271

Disney Magic-Business Strategy book, 20.00

Disney Magic Ideabook, 15.00

Disney Magic-Business Strategy audio cassettes, 89.00

Disney Magic-Business Strategy audio CDs, 99.00

Magic Moment Recognition Plan Starter Pack, 997.00

Check website or phone for current pricing.

SellBetter™

Quick Order Form

Fax Orders: 1-800-819-9087. Send this form.
Telephone Orders: Call 1-800-434-1291 toll free. Have your credit card ready.
Email Orders: orders@SellBetter.com
Postal Orders: SellBetter Tools, PO Box 50186, Phoenix, AZ 85076 USA.

Please send the following books, disks, or reports. I understand that I may return any of them within 90 days for a full refund of the purchase price for any reason, no question asked.

_____

_____

_____

Please send more FREE information on:

Other books   Speaking/Seminars   Consulting

Name:_____

Address:_____

City:_____State_____Zip_____-_____

Telephone:_____Fax:_____

Email Address:_____

Sales Tax: Please add 8.1% for products shipped to Arizona addresses.*

Shipping and Handling:
US: $4 for the first book or disk and $2 for each additional product.
International: $9 for first book or disk; $5 for each additional product (estimate).

Payment: Check   Credit Card:
   American Express   Optima   Visa   MasterCard

Card Number_____

Name on card_____Exp date:_____/_____
(Credit card orders must ship to credit card billing address.)
*Sales tax and prices subject to adjustment to current rates.

SellBetter™

Quick Order Form

Fax Orders: 1-800-819-9087. Send this form.
Telephone Orders: Call 1-800-434-1291 toll free. Have your credit card ready.
Email Orders: orders@SellBetter.com
Postal Orders: SellBetter Tools, PO Box 50186, Phoenix, AZ 85076 USA.

Please send the following books, disks, or reports. I understand that I may return any of them within 90 days for a full refund of the purchase price for any reason, no question asked.

_____

_____

_____

Please send more FREE information on:

   Other books   Speaking/Seminars   Consulting

Name:_____

Address:_____

City:_____State_____Zip_____-_____

Telephone:_____Fax:_____

Email Address:_____

Sales Tax: Please add 8.1% for products shipped to Arizona addresses.*

Shipping and Handling:
US: $4 for the first book or disk and $2 for each additional product.
International: $9 for first book or disk; $5 for each additional product (estimate).

Payment: Check   Credit Card:
  American Express   Optima   Visa   MasterCard

Card Number_____

Name on card_____Exp date:_____/_____
(Credit card orders must ship to credit card billing address.)
*Sales tax and prices subject to adjustment to current rates.

SellBetter™

Quick Order Form

Fax Orders: 1-800-819-9087. Send this form.
Telephone Orders: Call 1-800-434-1291 toll free. Have your credit card ready.
Email Orders: orders@SellBetter.com
Postal Orders: SellBetter Tools, PO Box 50186, Phoenix, AZ 85076 USA.

Please send the following books, disks, or reports. I understand that I may return any of them within 90 days for a full refund of the purchase price for any reason, no question asked.

_____

_____

_____

Please send more FREE information on:

Other books   Speaking/Seminars   Consulting

Name:_____

Address:_____

City:_____State_____Zip_____-_____

Telephone:_____Fax:_____

Email Address:_____

Sales Tax: Please add 8.1% for products shipped to Arizona addresses.*

Shipping and Handling:
US: $4 for the first book or disk and $2 for each additional product.
International: $9 for first book or disk; $5 for each additional product (estimate).

Payment: Check   Credit Card:
   American Express   Optima   Visa   MasterCard

Card Number_____

Name on card_____Exp date:_____/_____
(Credit card orders must ship to credit card billing address.)

*Sales tax and prices subject to adjustment to current rates.